KATE BUSH

The Biography

KATE BUSH

The Biography

Rob Jovanovic

PORTRAIT

Visit the Portrait website!

. . . .

PORTRAIT Portrait publishes a wide range of non-fiction, including biography, history, science, music, popular culture and sport.

If you want to:
• read descriptions of our popular titles
• buy our books over the internet
• take advantage of our special offers
• enter our monthly competition
• learn more about your favourite Portrait authors

VISIT OUR WEBSITE AT: www.portraitbooks.com

First published in 2005 by **Portrait**
an imprint of
Piatkus Books Ltd
5 Windmill Street
London W1T 2JA
e-mail: info@piatkus.co.uk

Reprinted 2005

ISBN 0 7499 5049 8

Text design by Paul Saunders
Edited by Andrew John

Typeset by Palimpsest Book Production Limited, Polmont, Stirlingshire
Printed and bound in Great Britain by MPG Books, Bodmin, Cornwall

Be kind to my mistakes

'Please don't call me the doctor's daughter from Kent and please don't call me an elf again. I get sick of it. I'm not an elf I'm a woman. I'm not the little goody-goody everyone thinks I am.'

KATE BUSH

Contents

Introduction

WHAT A LONG, STRANGE trip it's been. Like millions of others, I first recall seeing Kate Bush singing 'Wuthering Heights' on *Top of the Pops* way back in 1978. To be honest, I thought it was quite scary. To a nine-year-old she seemed to be some kind of ghastly apparition, an evil witch rising out of the dry ice. It wasn't quite on the level of behind-the-sofa, *Doctor Who*-type scariness, but it was unnerving. Of course, for teenagers and adults the viewing experience was quite unrelated, and, especially for the straight male audience, she aroused very different emotions.

Being scared of Kate Bush didn't last long, though, and soon she was a staple of British society and popular culture. Not long after that *Top of the Pops* debut my St Augustine's primary school friend – let's call him 'Phillip' to save any embarrassment – could be seen walking precariously on top of a high wall on the way home from school. All the while he'd be singing 'Wuthering Heights' in his prepubescent falsetto and dancing the elaborate choreography without falling six feet onto this head. It was quite a sight and, as is proved by my writing this, it left a lasting impression on me!

I didn't take much notice of Kate Bush for the next few years, but by the time I was at university I had a poster for *The Whole Story* on my wall and the same album on my record player. That 'best of' collection sold over a million copies, even though the British DJ John Peel allegedly said he couldn't take her seriously, and the respected American writer Dave Marsh once described her as sounding 'like the consequences of mating Patti Smith with a Hoover vacuum cleaner'. Praise indeed.

Kate Bush has fans across a wide spectrum of society. It's such a wide cross-section that a lazy journalist can easily find the more obsessive among the flock and paint the whole lot with the same brush. The press have generally been more kind to Kate herself. She, in the past, has been happy to play the publicity game in order to promote her work, but she has been intensely protective of her private life. She didn't officially acknowledge to the press who her boyfriend was for seven years, even though it was common knowledge, and no one knew she'd had a child in the 1990s until he was 18 months old. Generally, she's been left well alone.

The prospect of a book about her life and work is probably not welcomed at the Bush home, even though this volume isn't trying to find any closeted skeletons, make any wide-of-the-mark accusations or reveal where her son goes to school. Here you'll find a detailed look at her life and career. Though, as expected, she declined to be interviewed for this book, I have spoken with a wide range of producers, engineers and musicians to fine-tune a look at her recorded and filmed legacy.

Let's be open right from the start: she isn't a witch or mystical seer; she *is* arguably the UK's greatest ever female songwriting talent, though. She's a complicated person, just like everyone else, and she likes the old-time comedian Will Hay as well as Captain Beefheart and supersoaps such as *Dallas* as much as she admires the surreal artist Salvador Dali. Quite a combination. She draws her influences from music, cinema, television, dance and art. She's influenced almost every female artist of the last two decades in some way. Everyone from Alison Goldfrapp to P. J. Harvey, Björk to Martha Wainwright. Like the people she's influenced, she has a character that can take on many different hues. In 1986 she said, 'People spend their whole lives acting. You show this face to one person and another to someone else. It's all a form of acting. There are probably about twenty people in every individual. There is no one person at all – just lots of different characteristics.'

Let's take a look at them.

ROB JOVANOVIC
Isle of Arran
April 2005

Chapter One

Speaking For Me

London, December 2004

'I really like the idea of my work speaking for me. My work says a lot more intelligent stuff than I ever could and it's more eloquent.'

KATE BUSH

O N THE DAY IN QUESTION, it's been over three years since the world-changing events of 11 September 2001, but, if you didn't watch the news or read the newspapers, you'd think everything was pretty much back to normal. Whatever normal is.

As in most London winters of the past half-century, on this December day the capital is shrouded in a slow drizzly rain. It's not enough to be *that* noticeable, but enough to get you soaking wet if you're out in it for more than a few minutes. The pre-Christmas crowds shuffle along Oxford Street and the traffic is at a virtual standstill under the sad-looking Christmas lights.

If you ignore the cheap, touristy boutiques on Oxford Street, most of the stores are corporate chains that you could find anywhere up and down the country. It's nothing special, but the crowds flock to this centre of the metropolis anyway. Maybe there's a deep-down feeling of safety in numbers. If you were to mingle with the crowds you'd find that English tends to be the second language. When you do hear it, it's rarely spoken with an English accent.

Maybe, in the collective subconscious, the city's populace is keeping half an eye open for anything that seems suspicious, but that isn't something particularly new. Back in the 1970s it was the threat of the IRA that caused widespread paranoia. After two bombs exploded on the underground system, and a further seven went off in the West End, commuters and users of public transport were understandably edgy. Buses and tube stations were under close scrutiny (the latter had all their litter bins removed). So, in many ways, the atmosphere is unchanged now in the twenty-first century.

One thing that *is* different compared with almost 30 years ago is that you can't drive a car into the city centre any more without paying for the privilege. You could always use one of the famous red London buses, though, and save yourself some loose change. These same red buses have for as long as anyone can remember carried advertising around the city – often used to sell tickets to West End theatres or the latest Hollywood blockbuster movies. Today they are just as likely to carry banners advertising the latest pop recycling of a musical based on a 1970s band or singer as they are a bright new talent. But in early 1978 it was a wholly different case. Then, the buses paraded the fresh-faced, leotard-clad figure of an emerging young female singer who was taking the country by storm. Her name was Kate Bush.

After the hysteria that greeted her debut single, the once-heard-never-to-be-forgotten, 'Wuthering Heights', Bush proved herself to be arguably the most original and talented female singer of the next decade and a half. Then she suddenly dropped out of sight almost completely. Now, 26 years later, as those very London buses that had earlier paraded her face around the city trundle along Oxford Street, they pass music megastores that haven't been able to display a new Kate Bush album for the last eleven years. That's because she hasn't released one.

The late-2004 album charts could hardly be said to betray her influence on female music in the twenty-first century. Albums by Britney Spears (greatest hits), Shania Twain (greatest hits) and Tina Turner (greatest hits) were the only ones by female singers in the Top 20. But this lack of new music had hardly dimmed the perception of Kate Bush, not only among ardent fans but in the country in general. As time passed during the 1990s, she came to be seen as a kind of national institution or icon, to be revered and praised. She had been woven so deeply into the fabric of British life that music buyers in 2004, many of whom had barely been born when Bush originally burst onto the scene, could read the feverish rumours across the press and Internet that Bush had been in the studio. Or they could watch as an ageing football commentator pranced around on the BBC's *A Question of Sport* mystery guest slot dressed as the singer in her 'Wuthering Heights' video.

Back to our drizzly London afternoon, and Kate Bush was still everywhere, despite her attempt to withdraw from public life. On the Internet a myriad websites, chatrooms and discussion forums keep ticking along. On the airwaves, BBC Radio 2's Mark Radcliffe was running a campaign to get Kate to speak to him on his evening show (and ran a 'Bushometer' charting the time he'd been waiting for a reply), and the national press would occasionally send someone to try to track her down, get a candid photograph or try in vain for an interview. *Record Collector* magazine's annual poll voted Bush Number 1 Female Solo Artist, despite the massive gap since her last album. Bush had come to be hailed as the quintessential English singer and was always around in the country's cultural subconscious, bubbling just under the surface.

Other artists have taken time out and disappeared from view but few have had such a fervent following waiting with baited breath for their return. So what is it about Kate Bush that inspired such devotion and patience? Surely it wasn't just the old chestnut of 'absence makes the heart grow fonder'? At the end of 2004, a novel-cum-brief-biography of the singer was published under the title *Waiting for Kate Bush*. But where is she and what has she been doing? In the characterless world of twenty-first-century pop, it perhaps isn't surprising that someone so original is so craved for.

She'd been born into an upper-middle-class family. By the age of 17 she'd landed a record contract and at 19 had a Number 1 single. After following up with a successful tour and more high-riding singles, she could have easily slipped into the persona of a prima donna by the age of 21. She didn't enjoy the spotlight of fame and was well protected by an inner circle of family. Was she having her cake *and* eating it? To counter these silver-spoon-in-the-mouth images, she produced an amazingly broad scope of material, and proved naysayers wrong by exhibiting a series of vocal styles that steered her away from what was in danger of becoming a trademark image. She flourished in the new medium of the pop video and cast a shadow that reached far beyond the UK music scene. The list of artists and singers she influenced and inspired (seemingly everyone from Pat Benetar to the Scissor Sisters, Outkast to Tori Amos) hasn't even been enough to fill the void left by her absence.

In 2004 Q magazine's Icons Special Edition saw its readers vote Kate into 29th place among the Greatest Music Stars of All Time. Her incredibly loyal fan base meant that any new album would be a massive seller. But what would her reaction be to the attendant publicity? Would she do interviews? Tours? Videos? Speculation had been building for years, but then, on this December afternoon, Bush posted the following message to her usually very quiet fan club headquarters:

Hello Everyone, Many thanks for all your great letters of support and encouragement – they mean such a lot. The album is nearly finished now and will be out next year – we'll let you know when. It features some beautiful orchestral movements by

Michael Kamen – we had a wonderful day together at Abbey Road Studios last winter. I'm so pleased with everyone's work on this record. There are some lovely performances and I hope you will all feel it's been worth the wait. Bertie keeps me very busy, he is so much fun and we are all really looking forward to Christmas. Wishing you a Merry Christmas and I hope next year is a really happy one for you. Lots of love, Kate x

Such startling news caused pandemonium among the press, radio, TV and Internet sites. THE RETURN OF POP'S GREAT RECLUSE, exclaimed the *Daily Express*; COMEBACK KATE led the *Evening Standard*, which quoted an anonymous 'friend of the singer' as saying,

We've all been waiting for Kate to go back to the studio and show the world that she's still got the talent that made her such a star. It's no secret she's a very shy, emotionally frail person who's had her fair share of demons. We're all praying the pressure that comes with relaunching her career won't be too much for her.

The *Daily Mirror* weighed in with KATE'S BIG COMEBACK and pointed out her 'Miss Havisham-like existence behind the high walls of the mansion on the edge of the village' and her 'personal fortune estimated at £25 million'. The *Sun* – never one for understatement – shouted, 'This could be the biggest comeback since Lazarus.' More reserved titles such as *Music Week* and *The Times* also weighed in and *Time Out* added, 'The reclusive banshee of Olde Albion has confirmed that her first album since 1993 will be released.'

Anyone with even long-gone connections to Kate was quizzed on the subject, sometimes in the unlikeliest of situations. Drummer Stuart Elliott was interviewed in a church for BBC television's Sunday night religious programme *Songs of Praise*, and mentioned that he'd been recording drums on the new album; Peter Gabriel was promoting his *Play* DVD in Toronto and said, 'Kate had a son and lost her mom and I think that kept her occupied. I spoke to her quite recently in fact and she's just about finished on a new record. It is exciting. She's being a mom and loving it. So, if you like, music's gone from being full-time to being part-time, so that slows you down. She pointed out [she takes] even longer than I take!' Such was the fuss that Marc Almond's official website even had to put out a statement saying that Almond *hadn't* sung on the album. It said, 'He wishes he could confirm the rumour as Kate is one of his all time favourite artists and he looks forward to her long awaited new album, one of the big music events of 2005.'

Whether the new album would live up to the hype generated by 12 years of waiting was unlikely, but, in the meantime, this is Kate's story so far.

Chapter Two

She Was Learning Violin

Welling, Kent, 1958–71

ᴠ

'She was learning violin, and living with anyone who is learning violin is a miserable experience.'

JOHN CARDER BUSH

N O SOONER HAD THE CAR slowly pulled into the wide driveway of East Wickham Farm than the passenger door was open. As she got home from school, the 11-year-old Cathy Bush jumped out of her dad's car and dashed into the house. Dropping her school bags over the back of a kitchen chair she mumbled a 'Hello' to her elder brother and mother at the table, grabbed a piece of chocolate from the table and ran upstairs to change out of her school uniform. Moments later she appeared again, but this time she was straight out of the door and into the back garden of the farm, scampering across to the barn behind it. Here she found her current passion: an old church harmonium that was decaying but still just about playable. This was the highlight of her day, bashing her way through the couple of hymns that she'd picked up after being shown the basics by her father. But all too soon her time was up and she was being called in for tea.

★   ★   ★

It's not that surprising, considering her pedigree, that Kate Bush has been as successful as she has an artist. Her parents and older brothers have all been dancers, musicians or poets to some extent.

Kate's parents, Robert John Bush and Hannah Daly, were married in Epsom during World War Two. Robert, born in April 1920, had started out studying for a mathematics degree but, as the outbreak of war changed many things, it also changed his educational route, which now directed him to medical school. He graduated in 1943, the year in which he married Hannah.

Hannah, a farmer's daughter and originally from County Waterford, Ireland, was a nurse at Epsom's Long Grove Hospital. She had been by all accounts an excellent folk dancer back home on the Emerald Isle, winning several amateur competitions.

Bush family mythology tells us that the handsome, moustached Dr Bush also had some musical talent and sold the publishing rights to one of his compositions to fund an engagement ring for Hannah. A year after their marriage at St Joseph's Catholic church, their first child, John Carder Bush, was born. Eight years later, a second son, Patrick, was born. By then the Bush clan had moved the few miles to Welling in Kent, where Dr Bush had set up as a general practitioner. Welling was the perfect postwar model of English suburban life. It was ideally placed just out of reach of the grimy big city and tucked away from the main route of London to Dover and the Continent beyond.

It's easy to picture Dr Bush as a slimmer, English, version of James Robertson Justice (star of the 1950s *Doctor . . .* series of films). He was tall, sideburned and pipe-smoking, and didn't suffer fools gladly, but would show infinite patience in later years when fans would knock on his door.

The family moved into a sprawling, early-seventeenth-century home known as the East Wickham Farm. The farm would prove to be a most enchanting place for children to grow up, with its maze of outbuildings, a mouse-infested barn, a hideaway in the shape of a hayloft, and an outdoor swimming pool that had replaced the duck pond. High perimeter walls and large trees sheltered the farm from the world outside and the ample gardens were perfect and magical, and made safe play areas for the young family.

As in many farmhouses, the kitchen was the heart and soul of the property. Family and friends would drift in and out while conversations and debates raged around the big wooden table. Discussions would echo from the kitchen's tiled floors all over the house covering all manner of subjects. While the kitchen was the Bush hub, the sitting room was a place for quiet retreat and also housed the family piano, which Dr Bush would often play to relax.

On 30 July 1958 a third child arrived for the Bushes, this time a daughter, Catherine. Catherine, or Cathy, as she was known from an early age, was delivered at the Bexleyheath Maternity Hospital in southeast London. Cathy was brought up as a Catholic in the confines of the loving family atmosphere with her two older brothers to keep a lookout for her, as well as her paternal grandfather, who lived at the farm until the early 1960s. Both John and Paddy (Patrick) were now taking an interest in music and literature, so the young Cathy was immersed in a creative and arty atmosphere. Music was everywhere, and she couldn't help but absorb it. However, despite later going to Catholic schools, she didn't take to religion at all. 'It never touched my heart,' she later said. 'I would never say I was a strict follower of Roman Catholic belief, but a lot of the images are in there; they have to be, they're so strong. Such powerful, beautiful, passionate images! There's a lot of suffering in Roman Catholicism.'

What made more of an impression on the young Cathy was her mother's Irish heritage. From the stories of her mother's dancing exploits through to the Irish folk sounds that would saturate the house, Cathy soaked it all up, but she didn't get the chance to visit her mother's homeland until many years later. 'I feel that strongly, being torn between the Irish and the English blood in me,' she explained. 'The Irish influence is definitely very strong. My mother was always playing Irish music, and, again, I think when you are really young, things get in and get in deeper because you haven't got as many walls up. I watch her [Hannah], and when the pipes start playing everything just lights up and it can be so inspiring. It's just emotional stuff. I think I was really lucky to be given that kind of stimulus. It's really heavy, emotionally. The pipes really tear it out of your heart.

'My mother's picture of Ireland was of her home, and no further than that, literally. And that is where her heart is. And all her memories and the things she says of home are just beautiful. I think it has definitely affected my attitude toward Ireland. That's why I feel so at home, why I love it so much. I can feel my mother everywhere there.'

Cathy's earliest musical 'involvement' was as a small toddler just dancing to music coming from a TV set, totally oblivious of her surroundings. She can't really remember it but was told about it by her father years later. Away she'd go in her own little world until one day someone inadvertently came into the room and the shy little girl was caught unawares. She stopped the practice there and then. She did, however, enjoy dressing up in old clothes with her brothers, often to be photographed by John, but by the time she came to start at primary school John, being 14 years older, was off to university.

The bonds he would form while studying law would be important in Kate's later musical career. He made friends with Ricky Hopper, who would go on to a career working for various record labels; he met Dave Gilmour, who went on to join Pink Floyd. John had been writing poetry for some time and continued to do so while away from home. Cathy was most impressed by his writing, as any younger sister would be.

Cathy started at the local primary school in 1963. She had soon made a small group of friends who would sometimes come to the farm and play, but she didn't integrate completely into primary school life. Her own advanced musical mind and her spending lots of time with her much older brothers most likely helped her grow up faster than many other girls of her own age. 'School was a very cruel environment and I was a loner,' she says. 'I learned to get hurt and I learned to cope with it. My friends sometimes used to ignore me completely and that would really upset me badly. I wasn't an easy, happy-go-lucky girl because I used to think about everything so much and I think I probably still do. I was writing from the age of ten and I was never really into going to discos and dances and stuff. I never told anyone at school that I did that because I feared it would alienate me even more. I found it very frustrating being treated like a child when I wasn't thinking like a child. From the age of ten I felt old and I became very shy at school.'

Despite being shy, she wasn't a complete outcast by any stretch of the imagination. Friends would play with Cathy at the large Wendy house she had at the bottom of the garden or with her many pets. The barn and outbuildings were perfect places for games of hide-and-seek and they could use the hayloft as a retreat. John had graffiti-ed his poems all over the walls and the girls would regale each other with stories of the farm's legendary ghost.

Sometimes Cathy's friends would accompany the family when they drove down to their second home, a modest, seaside holiday house at Birchington near Margate on the south coast – something they would do every summer. Here they'd go walking and cycling.

Just after Cathy started at primary school, the family (minus John) had undertaken a much longer trip, this time to Australia. They toured the country for around six months. It's been suggested that this may have been a tester for possible emigration, but this has never been confirmed, and Dr Bush brought the family home and continued with his practice.

Back in Blighty, Cathy made her first tentative steps into the world of singing. But it wasn't a case of reciting 'Twinkle, Twinkle,

Little Star' at a school play. She took the plunge by joining in some family singalongs, which included, as she later put it, 'dirty sea shanties', along with some traditional Irish tunes and folk songs.

'I'm very proud of it,' she explained. 'I can't think of a nicer influence. Traditional music says a great deal about the country. English folk music is a lot different from Irish folk music, not only musically, but lyrically. That song "She Moves Thro' the Fair" sums up the Irish spirit. It's incredible, so moving.'

Bush is quick to acknowledge her debt to the music that filled her formative years at home and pays credit to the input of her brothers. While England was swinging its way through the 1960s the Bush brothers were taking an extra-keen interest in folk music, and when they were old enough both played in bands around the pubs and clubs. English and Irish folk music was a very different beast from what had hit the charts via Bob Dylan and Joan Baez. Folk clubs had sprung up around the country to play host to the likes of Martin Carthy, and later Sandy Denny.

Cathy would often sing harmonies with her brothers and of course heard all the records they played around the farm. 'I think it was important because, when you are very young, your mind is so open for new stimulus and direction,' she has said. 'I think it was given to me then, so I didn't really have to spend maybe ten years finding out what I was here for. I think that's been an important part of my life.' Early photos of Cathy, later published in a book by her brother John, show a tiny, frail-looking girl. She had everything she needed around her but wasn't spoiled. The family were fairly laid back and quarrels were very rare.

Cathy celebrated her eighth birthday on the day that England won the football World Cup by beating West Germany 20 or so miles from the farm at Wembley Stadium in July 1966. The farm was unlikely to have been much of a party zone, though, since none of the family have ever exhibited much of a sporting bent. Within a couple of years, however, Cathy was sitting at the piano plonking out some rudimentary scales. Paddy could often be found playing his violin around that time and it was suggested that Cathy could accompany him on the piano. This innocent suggestion inadvertently changed Cathy's life for ever. Dr Bush, who regularly played and composed at the family piano, showed Cathy how to play in the key of C, and off she went. In the very early stages she would practise on the old harmonium that was housed in the barn, so no one could hear her exploratory efforts. She was a diligent and determined student of the instrument and would spend hour upon hour pedalling away in the barn to a few old hymns that she'd been shown how to play. It wasn't long before Cathy had mastered the basics of playing a keyboard and would belt out the hymns in the barn. 'I really loved their melodies and harmonies and worked out myself that a chord was made from a minimum of three notes and by changing one of these notes you could get completely different chords to work with the new note.'

Over the years the workings of the harmonium were gradually devoured by the barn's mice and the thing became impossible to play, so Cathy had to move indoors to the piano. 'When [Cathy] began working on the piano, she'd go and lock herself away and wind up spending five or six hours, seven days a week, just playing the piano,' recalls Paddy.

Within a matter of a few months she was composing her own little instrumental ditties. Her father's interest in her playing proved to be a great boost to her enthusiasm. No matter how many times she asked him or how engrossed he was in a television programme, he would always agree to be dragged by his daughter into the sitting room to listen to her playing. 'I probably wrote the first song when I was about eleven, but, I mean, it was terrible, very overdone,' she laughs. 'I think the more you write songs, you just get a knack for them, hopefully!' Bush admits that, though her father would always listen to her playing, her parents weren't *overly* encouraging during her early experiments on the piano and that her voice was 'terrible'. In order either to encourage their daughter or to save their own ears – or both – the Bushes later sent Cathy for some voice coaching. She practised as often as she could because she saw it as the only way to improve.

The combination of practice and advice started to pay dividends and, by the time she moved up to grammar school after passing her 11-plus examination, she had a small catalogue of her own compositions.

Secondary school for Kate – she decided she'd outgrown the name Cathy – was at a Catholic convent school, St Joseph's in Bexley. So from September 1969 Kate was under the tutelage of the nuns. Not all the teachers were nuns, though, and not all students at the all-girl school were Catholic. The turn of the decade from the 1960s to the 1970s saw a softening of earlier hard-and-fast rules at the school. Not all things had been relaxed, however, and the strict uniform code of white blouse with maroon skirt and hat was strictly enforced. Any pupil found outside without their hat would be put on the Draconian-sounding 'hat-list' and two entries would mean an automatic detention.

The syllabus was a traditional one and Kate took a great interest in her English and Latin classes. She also expanded her musical repertoire by taking up the violin, though it wasn't by choice. All of the students were required to take up an instrument for music lessons but the piano was not an option so she was allocated a violin. Her parents paid for extracurricular lessons, again to save their own ears as an 11-year-old violin student is not the best of housemates. Again she was a dedicated pupil though piano would always be her first love.

In 1970 John Bush published a small booklet of his poetry called *The Creation Edda*. He was enjoying some success as a poet at the time and gave readings on the radio while having his work published in titles such as *Poetry Review*. A little later he organised a poetry group under the name of the Salatticum Poets. In another example of how Kate was influenced by her brothers she was soon sketching out poems of her own. During her first year at St Joseph's she had a poem titled 'Crucifixion' published in the school magazine and during her second year she had a whole series of them printed. Like that of her first-form effort, all of the titles seemed to have religious or spiritual connotations: 'I Have Seen Him', 'Death', 'You', 'Blind Joe Death' and 'Epitaph For a Rodent'. 'Call Me' goes like this:

> Call me and I will come,
> Across stones of memories
> And I will follow the sun,
> Blare, dare, they are others caring for none but . . .
> What of them?
> They are stones among children's hands
> Sighing crying, they, are, memories
> They are stones,
> Call me and I will come,
> Call me and I shall come,
> Tomorrow,
> What of tomorrow? Time rhyme,
> Through gates of glass, I would follow the sun,
> To run, to be free, to be me,
> I would flee, from corridors of cobwebs,
> Hold me!
> Call me!
> And I will come.

A natural progression for a girl who was composing some simple piano melodies and also writing poetry was to fuse the two together, and in 1971 she wrote several songs. One of these very early compositions was an early version of 'The Man with the Child in His Eyes'.

In 1972 she made her stage debut in the school production of *Amal and the Night Visitors*, but teachers were sceptical when they heard her play her own fledgling songs and it required input from her parents before her teachers would accept that her early tunes were entirely her own work. 'It's very hard to remember how I felt at the time, but it was something I enjoyed doing so immensely,' says Kate. 'It was my release from school, and if I couldn't go out and it was a wet day, or there wasn't anything good on television, that would be my favourite place to go: to the piano. I had such an excess of emotion that I needed to get it out of my system and writing was how I did it. It was a very important relationship and still is to me. I found something that I don't think I've ever really found since, when I first started writing songs: that I could actually create something out of nothing. And it was a very special discovery, I think, if you are lucky enough to make it at a young age, as I was.'

Kate was still exploring her brothers' musical and literary tastes and, though she was not a voracious reader, she did enjoy the work of the Narnia creator C. S. Lewis, the science-fiction great Kurt Vonnegut and the majestic poet T. S. Eliot. Musically, it wasn't all folk music, either: she grew to love classical music and composers such as Chopin, Debussy, Sibelius and Erik Satie. Around the kitchen table she would also be party to 'heavy' philosophical discussions across the spectrum of Greek mythology, the Armenian mystic Georges Gurdjieff, Kahlil Gibran and the music of the Beatles, T-Rex and the Incredible String Band. This semi-bohemian atmosphere might have been at odds with a traditional Catholic family background, but it didn't stretch into hippiedom, as Kate has had to say in her defence in interviews. 'I'm not a hippie, though I thought the potential of the movement was enormous. I was too young, really,' she explains. 'I was never particularly into drugs. I don't even get into alcohol very much. Just nicotine, really. I smoked my first cigarette at the age of nine.' So it wasn't just the piano playing that she started at an early age.

As well as adding some of her poems to her piano pieces, she also experimented with adding other people's words to her own music. Quite often she'd leaf through library books and pinch words or phrases that she liked. But she soon grew tired of this and she found out that it was actually easier to write her own words for the music than to try to artificially fit someone else's in.

'I couldn't read music at all,' she says. 'It was really a question of having a logical approach, once I knew where middle C was. Even though I wasn't much good at maths at school, I could see the logic of how the piano was working, and got on with it myself very well. I've now been playing the piano for many years, and I really did start off in the most basic way. After a couple of years I'd got a slight style, and since then I've simply developed it more, just by writing and then practising playing the songs.

'Often, I'd be writing songs beyond my technique, which would stretch my playing even further. Discovery of music personally for me came when one day my father took me in to the piano and showed me the scale of C on the keyboard. And I couldn't believe that this was how this worked, that it was so logical, that there was actually a plan to the keyboard that was so easy to see, that it was like playing one finger on the notes and then singing that tune. And then gradually I got to understand about chords, and once I hit chords that was really it, you know. This was the most exciting thing in my life, the chord.'

Luckily for Kate her family were very supportive, even when she was plonking away at the piano or hacking at the violin. 'I think I am most definitely a strongly emotionally-based person, and my family are totally integral, I think, to everything I do. They affect me because I love them. I think it's essential. I think it's something that has always been there, and that if it wasn't there it would probably be devastating for me.'

In the shadow of the likes of Laura Nyro and Joni Mitchell, she felt that a girl and a piano could make it, and the fledgling success of John Bush's published poetry no doubt proved to her that anyone could be successful if they had some talent. So, during the very early 1970s, she pushed on with her writing and keyboard practice, and soon she would start recording some of the songs that she'd written.

Chapter Three

We Had Quite Modest, Curious Aims

Welling, Kent, 1972–74

'[My family] had seen it coming for a long time. The original idea was to see if we could sell my songs to a publisher, not that I should be a singer or a performer or anything. We had quite modest, curious aims. So it was gradual and they were always supportive.'

KATE BUSH

AS USUAL, KATE SPENT the early evening on her own in the sitting room at the family piano. Sitting bolt upright, she effortlessly bounced from one idea to the next and ran through a selection of songs that she'd written for herself over the previous few months. She was still quite nervous about playing while anyone else was in the room, but of course the family had heard her songs resonating about the old building. Today she was totally unaware that listening behind the slightly open door was a guest of her brother John. This guest had been persuaded to come and listen to the gifted teenager at the piano in case he thought she might have any semblance of a future ahead of her in the music business, maybe as a songwriter for hire. If so, he might want to help; his name was Dave Gilmour and his band, Pink Floyd, was currently one of the biggest on the planet.

★   ★   ★

By 1972 the British pop charts had morphed into an unusually eclectic mix of genres and styles. Over the previous few months, Kate Bush's optimism would have been lifted by the fair share of piano ballads riding high in the charts (led by Simon and Garfunkel's 'Bridge Over Troubled Water' and John Lennon's 'Imagine'). Female singer-songwriters were also making a deep impression with all-time classics such as Joni Mitchell's *Blue* and Carole King's *Tapestry* (though English females were conspicuous by their absence). Heavy metal (Deep Purple), folk (Lindisfarne) and vacuous pop (David Cassidy) were all thrown into the mix, too, along with the new exciting sounds of glam, at the forefront of which were David Bowie playing as Ziggy Stardust, Slade and T-Rex.

Now 14 years old, Kate Bush was taking more inspiration from beyond her brothers' record collections and exploring more of these diverse sounds. She remembers early Roxy Music albums with much affection and an aura of newfound excitement. 'It was like, "Ah! This is *my* music, this is what I want to be associated with." It was such wonderful songwriting, very English as well, not American-style, and, of course Bryan Ferry's voice.' It wasn't just British voices that caught Bush's attention: Billie Holiday, Elvis Presley and Buddy Holly all found their way onto her turntable.

At home she was lucky in that as well as having a bedroom to herself she also had a room next door, which she called her 'den'. Stocked with comfy sofas, cushions scattered across the floor and of course her coveted record player, this was where friends could sleep over and hours could be spent listening to her records and 'borrowing' more from her brothers' collections.

'My other musical influences really have been things from the radio, because what you listen to are the things that are going on,' she recalls. 'I started seeking out my own stimulus and that came from people like Billie Holiday. She was a really important thing to happen to me. Her voice just really did things to me. So emotional and so tearing. I still can't get over how incredible her voice was and her presence. I was into more progressive people, I guess, like David Bowie and Roxy Music and Steely Dan. I think they're a very underestimated group, especially in England. They really are an important musical influence. I think the main common denominator for the people that I like is that they're songwriters. They all seem to be either male groups or male single personalities who write their songs and sing them. And I think this is why I tend not to listen to females as much because the few that do get this together I don't find particularly interesting. Joni Mitchell stands on her own. I think Joan Armatrading, too – she's special. But, on the whole, I think I just identify more with male songwriters.'

Then add to this collection the likes of the Beatles, Roy Harper and, a little later, the Boomtown Rats and Thin Lizzy, and she had quite a broad musical footing to draw upon for her own compositions.

One male singer-songwriter to whom she took an extra-special shine was Elton John, especially because he used the piano as his major composing instrument.

'He was just my hero,' Kate says. 'He's a fantastic piano player, a great performer. These people make a big impression on you. I had a bit of a crush on him. I thought he was fantastic, I thought he was so clever. It was before he got really famous . . . around *Madman Across the Water*. I thought he was so wonderful. I'd play the records and dream of being able to play like him, those fantastic hands.

'But a crush like that is quite sweet, isn't it? I had David Bowie on my wall as well. But he was the first great popular piano player I heard. I used to sit and listen to his records for hours. I wanted to be able to play like him, so I used to practise harder. I wrote [to him] saying how much I like him. I quoted some of Bernie Taupin's lyrics and told him how I played his music when I was low, and how much better I'd feel. I took it round to the BBC. I didn't know where else to send it. I don't suppose he ever got it.'

Like many teens, the 14-year-old Kate Bush was a heady mix of contradictions. By the time she reached the fourth form it was obvious that she was quite gifted academically but didn't really care too much for school or for progressing her education any further. John had been to university and Paddy to a London college, but she was distilling other ideas. She could be very shy and introverted at school but she also had friends over to stay and they'd be allowed to put on parties in the barn so long as they didn't get too rowdy or end up in the pool.

'I found [school] wasn't helping me,' she explains. 'I became an introvert. I guess it was the teachers' system the way they react to pupils and I wasn't quite responsive to that. I was an optimist, an idealist. That goes hand in hand with youth. You're either anarchic or optimistic. I had such positive attitude. I wish I had as much now as I did then. Some of the positivity is gone. But on the whole I'm more positive than negative. I'm never grumpy. I like to think I'm quite a happy little soul.'

St Joseph's, with its redbrick Victorian exterior and a stern school song called 'Death Before Dishonour', was perhaps all a bit too heavy for teenage Catholic school girls. Bush's attitude that formal education was meaningless with respect to her ambitions for the outside world is more understandable.

She, like millions of teenage girls, had her share of secrets. The biggest one was her music. Few, if any, of her friends knew how gifted she was or that she was even composing dozens of songs at home. She didn't want to stand out or appear to be 'cleverer' than her classmates, and in order to fit in she kept it all to herself. Because of this secrecy she couldn't really tell anyone outside her close family that she had serious thoughts of making music her career. When the time came to talk about careers at school she toed the party line and told her teachers she might consider training as either a vet or, more likely, a psychiatrist. If she chose to follow either profession she would have been able to draw on her father for help and advice. But deep down she knew it was just a pretext. In going through the motions, she spent a week at Newcastle Polytechnic to sample university life and have discussions about her possible career paths.

'I really wanted to be a psychiatrist,' she remembers. 'That's what I always said at school. I had this idea of helping people, I suppose, but I found the idea of people's inner psychology fascinating, particularly in my teens. Mind you, it's probably just as well I didn't become one. I would have driven all these people to madness. I'm better off just fiddling around in studios. The really important thing about music is that all it is is a vehicle for a message, whatever your message is. I'm probably a lot better at being a songwriter than I would be a psychiatrist, for instance. I might have people jumping out of windows now. Music is very much a therapeutic thing, not only for me. That's a really good word. It really is like a therapy. The message I would like people to receive is that if they hear it and accept it, that's fantastic. If they let it into their ears, that is all I can ask for; and, if they think about it afterwards or during it, that is even more fantastic. There are so many writers and so many messages, to be chosen out of all of them is something very special.'

In the confines of the farm Kate was writing at an ever-increasing pace and with ever more authority and confidence. Her brothers started to take notice that this was becoming more than just a teenage passing fad or occasional hobby and that her compositions were improving exponentially. By late 1972 and the spring of 1973 she had assembled a single-reel home demo of more than 20 songs and these were sent out to various record companies to test the water for any interest. Each of the songs featured just Kate and her piano. The feedback was not great. 'I could sing in key but there was nothing there,' admits Bush. 'It was awful noise, it was really something terrible. My tunes were more morbid and more negative. That was a lot of people's comment. They were too heavy. The old [songs] were quite different musically, vocally, and lyrically. You're younger and you get into murders.'

The earliest songs with known titles include 'The Man with the Child in His Eyes', 'Davy', 'Atlantis', 'Cussi Cussi', 'Need Your Loving', 'Sunsi', 'Something Like a Song', 'Gay Farewell', 'Disbelieving Angel', 'You Were the Star' and 'Go Now While You Can'. All but the first of these songs remain unreleased to this day. Others have leaked out in one form or another, though, and a revamped studio recording of 'Need Your Loving' was released as a B-side under the title 'Passing Through Air'. Eight others have been circulated by collectors for a number of years. It's most likely that, although these unofficial collections contain the same songs, they date from later sessions, when they were rerecorded.

At the end of the 1972–73 academic year Bush took her mock O-level exams. It's known that she got into trouble at school because she missed at least one of these while she was recording an early version of 'The Man with the Child in His Eyes'. In a recent interview, John Bush commented that family friend and singer Julie Covington paid for, and arranged, the first studio session that Kate ever played, so it's quite likely that these two events coincided. Covington had met John Bush while she was studying at Cambridge and had gone on to appear in numerous plays and musicals (she later had a hit single with 'Don't Cry For Me, Argentina').

'My family thought it would be interesting to see if we could get some of my songs published – I'd written loads of songs,' says Bush. 'I just used to write one every day or something. Of course, there was no response. You wouldn't be able to hear a thing, just this little girl with a piano going "yaaaa yaaaa" for hours on end.'

At around the same time, another of John Bush's Cambridge friends, Ricky Hopper, was asked by the family to try to place Kate's demo tape. He'd worked at Transatlantic Records for a while and had a few contacts in the music industry. It's lost in the mists of time now whether the family or Ricky Hopper was actually the first to send demo tapes to record companies but, either way, the result was the same: rejection. The idea had been for the tape to be used to gain a rudimentary publishing deal but the demos, and by now there were as many as 60, were too much for anyone to absorb in one sitting. Song after song of a young girl wailing away at a piano was not perhaps the best way to present Kate's new songs to a virgin listener.

A break in this tale had actually already occurred earlier in 1973 when Hopper got married. Through his work at Transatlantic Records he'd met a band called Unicorn. They'd released an album called *Uphill All The Way*. Hopper had done a few favours for the band in the past, so, when he asked them to play at his wedding reception, they agreed to do it for free. Unicorn put on a great show of folk-rock in the style of Crosby, Stills, Nash and Young. A guest at the wedding, and another friend from Hopper's Cambridge university days was Pink Floyd guitarist Dave Gilmour. At the end of the reception he climbed on stage, strapped on a guitar and suggested they all jam their way through the recent Neil Young hit single 'Heart of Gold'.

It's worth noting that in early 1973 Pink Floyd were about to become the biggest band in the world. When their album *Dark Side of the Moon* was released in March of that year it started an incredible run of over 700 weeks in the *Billboard* 200. Having morphed from the psychedelic sounds of the Syd Barrett-influenced line-up, their 1970s work was starting to take on a grandiose style that became a kind of classical rock opera that pushed all pop formats to the limit and gave instrumental music a massive lift.

Having returned from a US tour in June, the band split for a few months' rest, but Gilmour wanted to put his time 'off' to good use. He'd been toying with the idea of using his experience in the business to help get new acts off the ground. He got in touch with

Unicorn with an offer that they could come and use his newly installed home studio in Royden, Essex. Of course, they jumped at the chance and actually recorded with Gilmour there on several occasions. Later they also signed to Pink Floyd's manager Steve O'Rourke's management agency.

It was Hopper's 'reunion' with Gilmour at the wedding that later sowed the seeds of the idea that he might be able to get some help from the guitarist in placing the Cathy Bush tape with a label. Gilmour was sent a copy of the full demo tape and sat down to listen to it all the way through. Whether he managed to stomach it right through to the end is unknown, but he heard enough in what he did hear to capture his interest. The timing was great because Gilmour had a little bit of free time again from a busy schedule with Pink Floyd and was also in the frame of mind where he wanted to give artists a leg up the recording ladder if he thought they had some natural talent. Just as he had proved with Unicorn.

Gilmour had a musical ear capable of separating the wheat from the chaff, and decided that there was some real talent evident among the weaker tracks. He wasn't overly impressed with the presentation or the quality of the tapes, though, so he told Hopper he'd like to meet Kate and listen to her play live.

Shortly before Kate's 15th birthday, Gilmour drove down to the farm and secretly listened as Kate sat at the family piano ready to play her songs unaware that she was about to audition for a world-renowned superstar. Later she was told Gilmour was there and played for him some more. Bush wasn't exactly cool and calm about the prospect. 'I was absolutely terrified and trembling like a leaf,' she recalls. 'He came along to see me and he was great, such a human, kind, person, and genuine.'

During this recital Gilmour made a new lo-fi demo tape with fewer songs on – though how many is unknown – in order to try his own luck with a few labels. However, he soon found out that a slightly more professional approach was required, and so he invited Kate, a month after her 15th birthday, to come and play at his home studio and he'd provide a backing band to give her demos a little bit more 'oomph'.

Between Gilmour, Hopper, Kate and her family it was decided that a trimmed-down set of just three or four songs should be recorded and the ones that stood out for trial at Gilmour's studio were 'The Man with the Child in His Eyes', 'Passing Through Air', 'Davy' (a.k.a. 'Maybe') and perhaps one or two others. To date these have never been heard outside the Bush inner circle and are a collector's Holy Grail.

Unicorn bassist Pat Martin recalls that Gilmour called him and asked if he and drummer Pete Perrier could come and play on some demos. Martin had already heard about Bush from Ricky Hopper, who'd been waxing lyrical about her talents. Martin, Perrier and Gilmour set up their equipment about an hour before Bush was due to arrive and ran through a sound check to make sure everything was spot on for her arrival. She'd never played with a band before and they wanted to make sure that everything ran smoothly and that it was as undaunting for her as possible. The studio was well equipped with an eight-track recorder, 16-channel mixing desk and both an upright piano and a Wurlitzer electric piano for Kate to play.

When she arrived with Ricky Hopper, Martin recalls meeting 'a shy, beautiful schoolgirl with a dreamy look in her eyes and I remember her dimples when we got her to smile. She had never played with other musicians before and loved playing with bass and drums for the first time.'

On these tracks Kate played piano and sang, Gilmour played guitar and engineered and the Unicorn pairing of Perrier and Martin combined for the rhythm section. '[I was at] Dave's for a day, basically,' explains Bush. 'The bass player and drummer from Unicorn sat down and we just kind of put a few songs together. I remember it was the first time I'd ever done an overdub with the keyboard – I put this little electric piano thing down, and I remember thinking, "Ooh!' I like this!"'

The songs were recorded as a live band performance over a period of five or six hours. 'She had no idea how things were done and was very nervous,' says Martin. 'We told her to just play the songs and we put our own parts to it. She kept saying she was knocked out with it. Some time later, not too long, David recorded a load of her songs with just her and a grand piano. I remember he did it on a four-track Teac [recorder] in an office somewhere. At one point I had the four-track tape and there was loads of her early songs on it.

'When David moved from a storage place he had, they found lots of rare Floyd, Cathy Bush and Unicorn tapes. Some came out of their boxes in the move and got put back in the wrong boxes. I had boxes given to me marked "Unicorn" and when I played them they were live Pink Floyd shows, Cathy's four-track tape and the most pretentious interview I ever heard featuring Roger Waters. I gave them back to David straightaway but I reckon I could have made a fortune bootlegging them!'

Martin did make a small amount of money from this session, however. 'I only met her twice again,' he recalls, 'once when we were mixing some Unicorn stuff at AIR Studios and once she came into the Floyd's Britannia Row Studios. Rick Wright's keyboards were set up and I remember showing them to her and she was excited to have a go on them. She was still naïve and sweet. Years later, when "Passing Through Air" was used as a B-side, David sent Pete and I some session fees. We did the original session for free. He said Cathy's manager had expected him to give her the tapes for free but he insisted on Pete and I getting paid. I think we got about ninety pounds each, which was great, as we were very poor at the time, as Unicorn had been swept away by the New Wave.'

Exact details of where and when Gilmour made further solo recordings of Kate and her piano are unknown. The 1973 demos bootlegged under the title *The Early Years* most likely come from the 'office' session, most probably still in the late summer of 1973.

Many years later it looked as if a sensational LP version of the tracks from this (or maybe another early Gilmour) session were about to be released on an obscure German label. In 1986 they actually went ahead and pressed an unknown number of white-labelled promotional discs and distribution deals were being set up across Europe, while the German wing of EMI stood by and did nothing to prevent it. The small label had wrongly assumed that, because they had managed to buy physical copies of the tapes, they also owned the reproduction rights. Then, at the last moment, the plug was pulled on the project and its release was blocked. All the pressed discs were supposed to have been destroyed, although one was later listed for sale at a London auction house before being mysteriously withdrawn. The track listing to this elusive disc, tentatively titled *The Early Years*, is as follows: 'Something Like a Song', 'Need Your Loving' (a.k.a. 'Passing Through Air'), 'Davy' (a.k.a. 'Maybe'), 'You Were the Star', 'Gay Farewell', 'Cussi Cussi', 'Atlantis', 'Sunsi', 'Disbelieving Angel', 'Go Now While You Can'.

These early songs give a clear demonstration of how prodigious a talent she really was. Few people of her age would be capable of writing such mature material and have such an ear for a well-structured song. Bush's piano playing was also superb – it *had* to be, since it was the only instrument on these songs. Her voice rises and swoops through 'Atlantis' but is a little close to the edge on some notes and would be a little too screechy for those who found 'Wuthering Heights' hard to take. 'Sunsi' and 'Cussi Cussi' display a more level-headed vocal approach, and 'You Were the Star' is one of the best songs of the bunch. It certainly sounds good enough to have been progressed further and one can imagine a sweeping orchestral ballad coming out of this stark demo. 'Passing Through Air' was the only song to be commercially released from this selection, and it is one of the most authoritative vocal performances that Bush puts in.

When even the demos recorded at the Gilmour studio failed to generate any immediate interest, it was decided that Kate should step back a little from trying to get a publishing deal. She was about to enter the academic year of 1973–74, which would be her final year before her O-level examinations. So the search for a contract was put on hold to allow her to concentrate on her school work.

She didn't give up music completely during that year, though. She still played and wrote new material. 'I used to write poetry like everyone else did in English classes,' she says. 'Everyone was free to read them – we always read each other's work. But people at school didn't know that I was writing songs. At 16 I had gotten to the point where my songs were presentable. That was after five years of writing ballads and slow songs like "The Man with the Child in His Eyes".'

In the summer of 1974 she gained an impressive haul of 10 O-level passes and, with nothing better on offer, she decided to enter the lower sixth form at school and start her A-level studies. The usual route, of course, was O-levels (this was in the years before GCSEs), A-levels and then university, but Kate still had the idea of being a songwriter at the forefront of her ambitions. That summer's charts featured the sounds of Paul McCartney and Wings, Mike Oldfield's *Tubular Bells*, the last embers of progressive rock and the beginning of the end for the glam set. A whole new musical movement would soon take off in the form of punk, but, as Kate enjoyed the summer and wrote more songs, she was as far away from that new genre as could be.

Chapter Four

I Was Never a Girl Guide

Lewisham, London, 1975–77

'I was never a Girl Guide. I'm a bit of a loner. I love being with people but I've never been one for clubs. But again I was quite young when I began to do this work, so I was putting my energies into different things from what my friends were doing. Not that I missed out on a childhood or anything dramatic like that. But it was around the age that a lot of my friends were joining groups and going to youth clubs and discos.'

KATE BUSH

DURING THE HOTTEST BRITISH summer for 250 years, any use of public transport was hot, sweaty and unpleasant. But every day Kate Bush would catch the tube and travel by bus into London for her classes. She had coaching for her voice, as well as dance and mime classes. This was during a time when bomb scares were commonplace in the capital and everyone was watching stray plastic bags and wondering what might be in them. But public scares and the sweltering atmospheric conditions weren't enough to temper her enthusiasm.

★　★　★

Pink Floyd were very busy between the summers of 1973 and 1975. They'd been recording an album under the title of *Household Objects*, then shelved that idea and put down the majestic *Wish You Were Here* instead. European and UK tours followed in 1974, but Dave Gilmour managed to fit in the time to get married and then they toured the United States. After further North American tours in April and June, they returned to England in June 1975 for the Knebworth Festival. When all this activity began to simmer down, Gilmour decided it was time to have another go at getting Kate Bush some recognition.

After Kate's early home demos, followed by the band recording of the Gilmour home demos and the further solo 'piano demos', the next logical step, and perhaps the last chance at placing the tapes, was to set up some serious studio work with a recognised producer. Despite the previous setbacks, Gilmour was still confident enough to put his hand in his pocket and finance the sessions himself.

In June, just as Kate was revising to take her mock A-level exams, Gilmour booked a session for her at George Martin's AIR studios, just off Oxford Circus in London's West End. Using some of the best studio people around, Gilmore brought in Andrew Powell as producer/arranger and Geoff Emerick as engineer, while Gilmour himself worked in a producer role too.

AIR studios was a superb facility in the heart of London, which may have been a severe drawback with so much noise pollution and traffic vibrations. To overcome these potential problems the original AIR studios were built on the top floor of a building and housed on a bed of 'springs' so that the outside traffic noise and vibrations were dampened down and minimised.

Gilmour had full confidence in the 26-year-old Andrew Powell to make the most of Bush's precocious material. He'd had a varied musical education by working at an early age with the mercurial Stockhausen in Germany and then John Cage, not to mention more 'pop' work with Steve Harley and Cockney Rebel. Geoff

Emerick was well known because of his work under George Martin on some of the Beatles' most famous work, especially *Revolver*, *Sgt. Pepper's* and *Abbey Road*.

At AIR three songs were initially recorded with just Kate's voice and her piano playing: 'The Man with the Child in His Eyes', 'Saxophone Song' (a.k.a. 'Berlin') and 'Davy' (a.k.a. 'Maybe'). These were of much higher quality than 'mere' demo recordings. 'He put up the money for me to do that, which is amazing,' enthused Bush. 'No way could I have afforded to do anything like that. I think he liked the songs sufficiently to feel that it was worth his actually putting up money for me to go in and professionally record the tracks, because all my demos were just piano vocals and I had, say, like, fifty songs that were all piano vocals. And he felt, quite rightly, that the record company would relate to the music in a more real way if it was produced rather than being demoed. So he put up the money, we went into the studio, recorded three tracks.'

Gilmour assembled a makeshift band to play on two of the songs and for 'The Man with the Child in His Eyes' an orchestral section was brought in to complement Bush's plaintive piano ballad.

For 'Saxophone Song' the players were an experienced ensemble. Barry DeSouza (played with Lou Reed, Jeff Beck) on drums, Bruce Lynch (Rick Wakeman) on bass, Paul Keogh and Alan Parker on guitars, Alan Skidmore (John Mayall, Alexis Corner) on saxophone and Andrew Powell on keyboards. The result was an accomplished recording of a mature-sounding Bush, both lyrically and in her vocal performance.

Of the song, set in a Berlin bar, she says, 'Sometimes chord structures make you think of a place, and I love saxophones, so I wanted to write a song about them. I think of a beautiful sax like a sensuous, shining human being. It's vibrating, a very sexual sound, resonating, like bowels. If you look at photos of musicians, often they're cuddling the instrument. It's seducing you and you are seducing it. But it's so innocent.' The song starts out like many of her early songs with a ballad-paced voice and piano. Halfway through the first verse the band kicks in and Skidmore's sax takes over in the chorus. Powell's keyboards see out the track during an elongated instrumental ending.

But it was 'The Man with the Child in His Eyes' that made people really sit up and listen. 'The inspiration was really just a particular thing that happened when I went to the piano,' says Bush. 'The piano just started speaking to me. It was a theory that I had had for a while that I just observed in most of the men that I know – the fact that they just are little boys inside and how wonderful it is that they manage to retain this magic. I, myself, am attracted to older men, I guess, but I think that's the same with every female. I think it's a very natural, basic instinct that you look continually for your father for the rest of your life, as do men continually look for their mother in the women that they meet. I don't think we're all aware of it, but I think it is basically true. You look for that security that the opposite sex in your parenthood gave you as a child.'

The song was given a new dimension – to set it apart from the other piano ballads she'd recorded – when David Katz was contracted to bring in classical players for the orchestration, which lifted the song away from the nondescript morass of all her other ballads. Again the song started with an understated piano and horn motif, which goes into a wondrous bridge to the chorus. The chorus vocal itself is chased by Bush's piano motif and a lone flute. The overall effect is stunning and appears to be from someone well beyond her years.

Pink Floyd were signed to EMI records and Gilmour thought that they would be a good match for Kate's material. A short time after the AIR session, while Gilmour was at Abbey Road working on the *Wish You Were Here* album, he passed a cassette of the songs to the general manager of EMI's pop division, Bob Mercer. Pink Floyd had now reached such a level that, if Dave Gilmour suggested that you listen to a tape, you listened.

'If you see something that you think is brilliant,' says Gilmour, 'and particularly if that thing is being presented in such a way that most cloth-eared record company people wouldn't notice if it hit them falling off the top of a truck, then I sometimes feel a certain sense of responsibility to bring out what I think is good and then bring it to their attention. This is what I did with Kate. Her home demos were of her sitting at a horrible piano, recorded with a very ancient tape recorder, and her squeaking away. I listened to them and I could hear the talent but wouldn't have dreamt of taking them to a record company. I knew the only way to do it was to tart them up, if you like. We recorded her properly, with a proper producer and the best engineer, Geoff Emerick, arranger, and chose three or four songs out of about fifty, and made a proper record and presented it to EMI. And of course they said, "Great, we'll take it."'

EMI were keen on the tape but the deal wasn't sealed as quickly as Gilmour says above. 'I was in the Number Three studio of Abbey Road,' recalls Mercer. 'Pink Floyd were finishing off their *Wish You Were Here* album. Dave Gilmour asked me to nip into one of the studios and listen to a tape he and Andrew Powell had done of this girl. There were three songs on the tape. They seemed well produced. I expressed a lot of interest in it. When Steve, Pink Floyd's manager, came round to see me a few weeks later, I mapped out a deal. Then Steve said he wasn't going to be involved as a manager. So I asked Kate and her father to come and see me and mapped out a deal to them.'

EMI were one of the world's largest labels. Having originally started out as the Gramophone Company at the end of the nineteenth century, they had built up a reputation based on music hall, then classical music. After a merger with the Columbia Gramophone Company in 1931, they became Electric and Musical Industries or EMI for short. Shortly afterwards, the new company opened the world's first purpose-built recording studio at Abbey Road in London. By the 1970s they boasted a roster that included heavyweights such as Pink Floyd, Queen, Deep Purple and Iron Maiden.

Mercer opened negotiations with the Bush family and wanted to sign Kate as a recording artist, not just to a publishing deal. It was not an easy contract to arrange, though, since both parties agreed that Kate needed time to mature and develop before being thrust into the limelight as a solo recording artist. In the meantime Kate went back to school for the second year of her A-levels while meetings and discussions about her future continued.

'On meeting her I realised how young she was mentally,' says Bob Mercer. 'We gave her some money to grow up with. Over the next year I developed her, got her to demo everything she'd done, talked to her about the way she constructed her songs, and so on, and encouraged her to explore other things. We also got her a singing tutor.' It soon became clear that, because of Kate's age and the wishes of her family, it wouldn't be a usual deal in which the artist signed a contract for a given number of albums. Things were uncertain over Kate's continuing at school, too, but she carried on into the upper sixth form.

Word of this new prodigy soon spread around the offices of EMI. Terry Slater was working there at the time and he recalls, 'I was just passing by Bob Mercer's office one day and I heard a demo tape of "The Man with the Child in His Eyes" and I said to Bob, "Who's that chick?" I literally opened the door to the office and said that to Bob.' Slater got Kate's telephone number and called her in to speak with him. She went in the next day and, as Slater recalls it, she was just totally overwhelmed that somebody was interested in her music.

After much toing and froing a deal was finally agreed. She was to be given a £3,000 advance for a four-year contract, but EMI had the option of terminating the deal at the end of either the second or third year if they thought she hadn't developed as they hoped she would. She also received a further £500 from EMI Publishing. The deal was signed in July 1976, just as she was turning 18, and, with an inheritance that Kate received from an aunt that same year, she decided that she should halt her education before taking her A-levels. She also broke up with her first serious boyfriend. She'd been seeing a young biker from the leather-jacket crowd for about a year. When she played him her early demos she was typically so shy that she had to leave the room while he listened to them. She didn't look back, though, and neither did her school-mates. There's just one mention of her on the Friends Reunited website, where she's referred to as 'The Welling Warbler'.

She now had enough funds at her disposal to be able to leave home and start serious, full-time, preparations for the career that she'd been dreaming of for the past five years. For their part, EMI, or at least Bob Mercer, should receive some credit for the delicate handling of the situation and having the faith to reward an up-and-coming talent with some time to grow, something that just would not happen today.

'I came in to EMI on a friendly basis,' says Bush. 'That was good for me, because it meant that I could meet people there as people, and not as a big vulture business where they're all coming in and pulling your arm out. Also, I could learn about the business, which is so important, because it is a business.'

Another major 'developmental' step was Kate's moving out of her parents' house. This was done partly to increase her inde-pendence and maturity but the other part of the reason was simple logistics. She'd been spending hours travelling from Welling to dancing and singing classes and a move to the edge of London made life much easier in respect of the travelling she had to do. Like the somewhat unusual contract she negotiated with EMI, her leaving home wasn't as big a leap into the unknown as it might have been. She moved several miles from her parents' home to Lewisham, where her father owned a house that was split into three apartments, and Kate took the top one. The other two flats just happened to be occupied by her brothers Paddy and John. She called her flat 'very ordinary' but she was happy to have all of her things in one place and to be able to work on what she wanted, when she wanted.

So with her inheritance plus EMI's advance, a place to live near her brothers and no real worries about having to find a job, she was free to concentrate on honing her music and dance. Hannah and Robert Bush had the utmost faith in their daughter, secure in the knowledge that her brothers could keep and eye on her and that she was fully committed to working hard at things, and not just coasting along spending her windfall.

'The money did enable me to think that I could do it, because I was obviously worried about leaving school and finding myself nowhere,' she recalls. 'I had strong feelings in not having little securities like a nice little job. I wanted to try to do what I wanted and, if it went wrong, OK, but at least try to do it. I think when you leave school and you don't know what you're going to do, I was very much throwing myself to fate. If it hadn't worked, I would have been in a very difficult situation. I just worked very hard and hoped that I'd be able to make something of it and I was very lucky. I felt I had to leave school and just go for it. If I didn't make an attempt to throw myself into that lifestyle, I didn't feel it was something that was going to come to me. It's something you have to go out and get.'

At the apartment she bought a fairly cheap, second-hand, piano and continued to write as she had done at home, often in short spells of one new song per day. Even if it didn't come easily on a particular day she usually managed to come up with something, even if it was just a part of a melody or a single line of a lyric. 'I had such a routine going,' she says. 'It was get up, play the piano, go dancing, come back, play the piano, write songs all night, then go to bed. It was like that every day. I think it was one of the happiest times for me as a person. I'd just left school and I was beginning to find myself as an individual. It was very exciting, but I wanted more than anything in the world to make an album, just to see that piece of plastic.'

She also started forming some musical bonds with other musicians, many of which would last for decades. One of these meetings was with a local drummer. Back in 1974 a young, self-taught drummer by the name of Charlie Morgan had answered an advert in the music magazine *Melody Maker* asking for a drummer to join a new band. The band was Conkers and also featured Brian Bath on guitar, Ivan Penfold on guitar and keys, Del Palmer on bass and Barry Sherlock on keys and vocals. The band secured a record deal and went out on a college tour.

'We also played some local gigs,' recalls Morgan. 'Mainly in the southeast London area. I can tell you, we had a lot of fun. I also learned a tremendous amount about studio techniques. We rehearsed down in the basement at Cube Records next to their studio, and I started doing sessions for other writers that were signed to them.'

But after what Morgan refers to as 'our untimely demise at the hands of an inept manager and a lethargic record label' the band went their separate ways. But then, in late 1976, Del Palmer gave Morgan a call and said he had someone he wanted the drummer to meet.

'I remember driving to a flat on Kidbrooke Park Road, in Shooters Hill, which was a cross-town journey for me, being a Chiswick boy,' says Morgan. 'That's where I met Kate. She was very young, then. She and Del asked me to help form a band to back up Kate. Well, I was extremely interested, but had just signed a deal with a band that was signed to Island and respectfully declined. She was utterly entrancing! I knew she had something utterly unique. Apart from Kate's incredible personal magnetism, and the fact that she behaved so much older than her tender years, the music had so many levels, and the lyrics were "out there".'

The summer of 1976 was one of the hottest on record. On 26 June, London hit 35°C (95°F), while reservoirs up and down the country were consumed in the drought and left to look like parched deserts or lunar landscapes. Water rationing was severely enforced and, when rain eventually stopped play for 15 minutes at Lord's in August, the crowd gave the heavens a standing ovation. In this suffocating atmosphere Kate would be up late well into the early hours, singing and writing through the night with windows wide open to the sweltering city outside.

'I had all the windows open,' she laughs. 'I just used to write until, you know, four in the morning, and I got a letter of complaint from a neighbour who was basically saying *"Shuuut uuuup!"* cause they had to get up at, like, five in the morning. They did shift work and my voice had been carried the whole length of the street, I think, so they weren't too appreciative.

'I feel as though I've built up a real relationship with the piano,' she says. 'It's almost like a person. Like, it's really comforting just to sit down and play it. And the piano almost dictates what my songs will be about. If I haven't got a particular idea I just sit down and play chords and then the chords almost dictate what the song should be about because they have their own moods. Like, a minor chord is very likely to tell me something sad. A major chord tells me something a little more up-tempo and, like, on a more positive level of thinking. If I ever made enough money I'd like to get a piano that sings: a great big singing beast like a Steinway.'

Kate was a very determined girl and was intent on using the time she'd been afforded as shrewdly as possible. Singing, mime and dance classes were all undertaken in order to improve her position as an all-round performer. Though she describes her singing lessons as not being 'formal training', Bush did see a voice coach every week. They'd go through her scales and he'd give advice and tips on her breathing techniques. She'd sing her new songs for him and he'd help out on a song-by-song basis with how she could get the best from her voice in different situations. 'There was a guy that I used to see for half an hour once a week,' she recalls. 'He would advise me on things like breathing properly, which is very important to voice control. He'd say things like, "Does that hurt? Well, then, sing more from here [motions to diaphragm] than from your throat." I don't like the idea of "formal" training: it has far too many rules and conventions that are later hard to break out of.'

Kate would also spend many hours at home working on her scales. A large part of Kate's vocal progression came from just plain old hard work. 'I've always enjoyed reaching notes that I can't quite reach,' she explains. 'A week later you'll be on top of that note and trying to reach the one above it.'

For her dance and mime work it was more difficult to acquire the tuition she required. Having had no prior dance training and certainly no ballet qualifications she found it hard to find a place that would take her on for lessons. Part of this problem stems from her not getting on with her dance teacher at St Joseph's, so she'd neglected her studies, and now she had a lot of catching up to do.

Initially she found a mime class near the Elephant and Castle in London and during 1976 she attended Adam Darius's classes there once a week. Originally a ballet dancer, Darius had evolved his work into a fusion of dance and mime. Over his long career he has now worked with such varied performers, singers and film-makers as Kate Beckinsale, Ingmar Bergman, and Placido Domingo.

'[Kate Bush] was very intelligent and sensitive,' recalled Darius. 'She had the most expressive face and she absorbed the mime and training like a sponge. I teach so many people it's difficult to remember them but she was set apart in her seriousness. I remember that her immersion was unusual for a once-a-week student.' Bush would always ask lots of questions after the class, presumably so she could learn more quickly and practise her moves at home. Just as she'd later ask many questions in the studio, she had to know every in and out of a process, how everything worked and why. Mime and the very strong facial expressions that she learned here would be useful to her later video and film work throughout her career, and it's an art form that she is passionate about defending. 'I wouldn't call it an upper-class thing at all,' she says. 'It's probably further away from the upper class than anything else, because they probably find it hard to be free, as they're so caught up in all their status problems, and the same probably goes for working-class people in a lot of ways because they always feel this alienation from other people.'

Also in 1976, Bush saw an advert for Lindsay Kemp's *Flowers* production and an advert for his classes, which promised 'living fabulously through your senses'. Kemp was known as a controversial character, but had been described in the press as 'one of the greatest stage creatures this country has ever produced'. He'd started out as a self-taught ballet student before forming his own company in the 1960s and hooking up with David Bowie. Bowie's attraction to the weird and wonderful side of performance art naturally drew him to Kemp and Kemp would play Bowie's albums while running his dance classes. Five years later Kemp's influence on Bowie was complete when the Ziggy Stardust character emerged.

'Once I'd seen *Flowers*,' says Bush, 'I knew I had to do something which would be my own *Flowers*. Not necessarily a show. I remember it so well. I thought that, if one person could actually produce the music themselves and give him- or herself physically at the same time, then you'd get double energy coming from one person. It could only be stronger, and I thought, "Golly, that's what I want to do."' It was a lesson she learned well and certainly carried it on to her only performances a few years later.

She signed up for Kemp's classes at a Fulham church hall right away and he became a huge influence on her style. The informal classes, costing just 50 pence a time, were certainly good value for money. Kate expanded her repertoire with expansive arm movements and facial expressions.

'Marcel Marceau [the famous French mime] – I admire his stuff, but it's a little too staid for me,' Bush explains. 'It's the art of illusion, it's not really the actual showing of emotion, which is really what Lindsay teaches. And for me that's perfect because it's what music and any form of art is about: it's emotion, it's from inside. He taught me that you can express with your body, and when your body is awake so is your mind. He'd put you into emotional situations, some of them very heavy. Like, he'd say, "Right, you're all now going to become sailors drowning, and there are waves curling up around you." And everyone would just start screaming. Or maybe he'd turn you into a little piece of flame.'

It took a while for Kemp to notice Bush, but once he did he didn't forget her. 'I met Kate Bush like I meet many people, like so many of my friends, like I met all my company, and that was in classes at the Dance centre,' he recalls. 'The classes were very, very large, and I think that by the time she spoke to me she was terribly nervous. It was one tea break and she explained that she'd already had about a dozen classes with me, and I must say I hadn't noticed her at all. The classes were that large and she was the type of girl, child almost, that stayed at the back. After that I began to notice her more. I saw this tiny shining thing. She reminded me of Tinkerbell or Wendy or something. She gave everything in class. From that tiny, frail, shy person came this fabulous amount of drama. She loved the drama.'

Kemp later offered her a job in his wardrobe department for the presentation of *Mr Punch* at the Roundhouse Theatre, London. It was soon afterwards that he discovered she was being groomed by EMI and didn't need the money. She was very humble about it all and he'd had no idea of the path she was on. 'He fills people up,' enthuses Bush about her teacher. 'You are an empty glass and glug, glug, glug, you're full of champagne!'

Such was Kemp's lasting impression on Bush that she later penned a song about him ('Moving'), even though he left for Australia after she'd been his pupil for just six months.

Kate soon found another class willing to take her, as she didn't want to lose the momentum that she'd built up with Kemp. This time she joined Arlene Phillips's classes at the Dance Centre in Covent Garden. Phillips was an experienced teacher and was the choreographer for the dance group Hot Gossip on TV's *The Kenny Everett Show*. Since then she's worked on countless movies (*Annie* and *The Meaning of Life* to name but two) and stage musicals, (*Starlight Express* and *Saturday Night Fever*). 'I loved that,' says Bush of the Phillips classes. 'It's the only place you can go and learn to dance without qualifications, which I didn't have. You pay by lesson, and, even though I had never danced before, I did make great progress.'

Throughout 1976 and early 1977 she was also writing new material and made at least two new demo tapes. Many of these recordings have leaked out over the years and early treatments of songs that would later be recorded for her first two albums can be appraised. The largest collection of such recordings came from what has become known as the 'Phoenix Broadcast'. In 1982 the Phoenix, Arizona, radio station KTSM aired 22 of Kate's demo recordings. The DJ for the show was one John Dixon, who had earlier worked for EMI when Kate was working on her debut album. The song titles he read out during the show are now taken as the actual titles given to them by Kate herself, not, as often happens on bootlegs, just some names dreamed up by the bootleggers themselves. The tape he played may have been compiled from several different sources, as it contained songs from each of her first two albums and 17 songs that have never been officially released. Several of these song titles date back to the earliest 1973 recordings and so it can be deduced that they were still being considered by Kate after she'd signed for EMI. These tracks were initially bootlegged on a series of vinyl EPs called *The Cathy Demos* in 1989. 'Rinfey the Gypsy' (a.k.a. 'Playing Canasta in Cold Rooms') is another slow song, full of longing for a lost love and a broken promise of marriage; 'Snow' lets Bush display a little more than just the higher vocal registers; 'Something Like a Song' is the pick of the unreleased early songs as Bush explores some subtle textures of her singing, but it's a little short of lyrical. She also manages a little more variation in her piano playing, which after one has listened to a dozen similar tracks, can get a little boring. It's apparent why record labels found it hard to stomach long tapes with dozens of samey songs on them during her early attempts to get a deal.

Other demos showcase songs written during her apprenticeship, and give a rare glimpse of the basic recordings that were transformed for the first album. Early versions of 'Moving', 'Don't Push Your Foot on the Heartbrake', 'Kite', 'L'Amour Looks Something Like You' and 'Strange Phenomena' have all been circulated.

These were the first full-band demos to leak out from the Bush camp and show both how she had matured as a writer and how her songs took on a new life of their own when not just played on a piano. The basic band arrangement for 'Don't Push Your Foot on the Heartbrake' sounds like a live-in-the-studio take, with a pretty tight rhythm section and a good vocal. 'Kite' bounces along nicely, as it would on the finished album. 'L'Amour Looks Something Like You' is stark and a little tinny-sounding, with Bush's vocal coming across as too operatic. 'Strange Phenomena' badly misses the final studio atmospherics, sounding empty and quite pedestrian in this stripped-down form. A new song that was included on this demo tape was called 'Scares Me Silly' (a.k.a. 'Really Gets Me Going'). An upbeat number, it opens sounding like a Patti Smith song that outdoes 'Don't Push Your Foot on the Heartbrake' (which Bush referred to as her Patti Smith-type song) and it's a mystery as to why this song was never released anywhere, even as a B-side. Layered harmony vocals and a strong piano motif help switch from the plodding chorus to the completely opposite exuberant verses. This shift in dynamic is not quite on the scale of a Nirvana song but does make it an interesting composition nonetheless.

It's likely that these band demos were played by a loose ensemble of players who had come together to make music and allow Kate to practise with a real band rather than the musicians who would later play on Kate's debut album. Paddy Bush rounded up his old friend Del Palmer to play bass, Brian Bath (ex-member of Tame Company, Shiner and Conkers) on guitar and Vic Smith to play drums. Paddy would help out with the equipment and the elaborate – for a bar band, anyway – stage effects, such as a lighting system and dry ice. They planned to play the local pubs and bars to give Kate the experience of singing before a live audience. To keep the customers happy they worked up versions of some popular cover versions and agreed that they might pop in one or two of Kate's original songs if things went well.

'I just had this impression that she must be older and more mature,' recalled Del Palmer. 'Then at our first rehearsal – Kate, Brian and me, and a fellow called Vic Smith on drums – I felt a little nervous because I felt a particular emotional involvement coming on right from the word go. But I also just thought, "This girl's just eighteen", whereas I'd been struggling for years on my bass. And I knew I just had to get involved some way because this was going to be mega. It was a phenomenon because it was so completely different from what anyone else was doing.'

'Kate is a real English girl,' said EMI's Terry Slater at the time. 'She's from the roots of Great Britain. It's not a gimmick or produced. She's the first really English girl singer for some time.'

Never was Kate's Englishness more evident than on a moonlit night in early 1977. Very few places in the world could conjure up such an enigmatic yet widely popular piece of pop music while all around it was either disco or punk. On the night in question Kate managed it.

On 5 March that year, there was a full moon over London. On or around this night Kate took a break from rehearsing with what was now known as the KT Bush band and was messing around with a few ideas for a new song. She hadn't written much during the preceding couple of weeks, as rehearsals were taking up much of her time when she wasn't at any of her classes. She had a first verse and a chorus, but the whole thing seemed cyclical and she couldn't get out of the chorus. Around midnight as she sat at her upright piano, she paused for inspiration and, as she gazed out of her apartment window, it came to her – and she completed the song that she called 'Wuthering Heights'.

'There was a full moon and the curtains were open, and every time I looked up for ideas I looked at the moon,' she recalls. 'I had originally written something more complicated, but I couldn't link it up, so I kept the first bit and repeated it. I was really pleased.'

Wuthering Heights was, of course, originally Emily Brontë's novel, written in 1845–46, but Kate knew the story from seeing part of a film adaptation on TV. She'd read only a small part of the book when she wrote the song. Bush later explained that the song covered only the end of the story and the part that she had seen on the television. 'It's about the end of the film where Cathy has actually died and she's coming back as a spirit across the moors to come and get Heathcliff again. It just struck me very strongly because it shows a lot about human beings and how if they can't get what they want, they will go to such extremes in order to do it. This is exactly what she did. She wouldn't even be alone when she was dead. She had to come back and get him.

'I just found it really amazing. I thought the story was so strong. This young girl in an era when the female role was so inferior, and she was coming out with this passionate, heavy stuff. Great subject matter for a song. It was a real challenge to précis the whole mood of a book into such a short piece of prose. Also, when I was a child I was always called Cathy, not Kate, and I just found myself able to relate to her as a character. It's so important to put yourself in the role of the person in a song. There's no half measures. When I sing that song I am Cathy.'

'Wuthering Heights' aside, Kate went back to spending most of her free time practising with the new band. After a month or so of rehearsing, it was time to take the plunge and see what reaction a south London pub crowd would give to a bar band backing a pretty young girl who was belting out a selection of cover versions. The KT Bush band made its debut in April at the Rose of Lee pub in Lewisham. A sparse crowd of locals numbering fewer than a dozen (and that included brother John and father Robert) watched the show, which included classics such as the Rolling Stones' 'Brown Sugar', 'Satisfaction' and 'Honky Tonk Women', Marvin Gaye's 'I Heard it Through the Grapevine', and the Beatles' 'Come Together' and 'Sweet Soul Music'. 'I do love singing other people's songs,' she says. 'But I feel that that is in fact cheating because there are so many good singers around who sing other people's songs and there aren't as many songwriters in comparison.'

Paddy Bush made recordings of several of these early shows but they have never found their way into the hands of bootleggers. Several shows were played at the Rose of Lee pub and word went round that the KT Bush band were actually pretty good. 'I think maybe about the fifth or six week, you couldn't get in,' says Paddy Bush. 'And this was all before the album was released or anybody knew anything about Kate. The night she first did "James and the Cold Gun", that was really good.'

As Kate and the band grew in confidence they slotted in a few more of Kate's songs. 'I really enjoyed it,' she says. 'It was just the experience I wanted at that point. I was looking for things that would take me further into where I wanted to go, which was the music business and I'd been training as a dancer and this felt like the perfect stage, really, to go into a live situation.'

On Friday, 3 June, they played a show in Putney but hadn't thought much about the big England-versus-Scotland football match due to be played at Wembley the following afternoon. Thousands of Scots had travelled down for a few drinks on the night before the game and pubs around the capital were inundated with Scottish revellers. So the KT Bush band were faced with a pub full of slightly-worse-for-wear Scottish football fans with their homemade banners, scarves and flags decorating the pub. It can't have been the easiest show to perform, as the fans were more intent on wandering around the stage and giving Kate a good-natured kiss than listening to the music. But the atmosphere was friendly and passed without any real incident. Unfortunately, the same can't be said of the game the following day. After Scotland's 2–1 win, their fans infamously invaded the pitch, snapped both goalposts and dug up sections of the pitch to take home as souvenirs. Sounds like the KT Bush band got off lightly!

'I think one of the really interesting things was comparing live work with actually recording,' Kate says. 'It's such a completely different process, because, when you're gigging, which I did for a little while with my band, the KT Bush Band, we were just doing pubs around London. We were singing other people's songs. It's really different because you feed back off the audience. You can see their faces. You can tell if they hate you or if they love you. All you're trying to do when you're on the stage is to excite them, get them to have a good time and enjoy it. They need to know the songs and they need to be able to drink their beer and dance.'

In July, after three months of playing live, the original KT Bush band broke up because Kate had more pressing tasks at hand. The live shows had proved to be a vital part of Kate's development and the year had been spent wisely with voice training, dance classes, mime work and the first performances of her own material in front of a live audience – all giving her a greater sense of confidence. She'd also collected a strong body of work now and EMI clearly thought the time was right, because they called her up to go into the studio and record her debut album. Colin Miles was artist relations manager at EMI's subsidiary, Harvest Records.

'Once she was signed,' Miles recalls, 'a lot of people at EMI heard her voice, which was unique by any standards, and were far from convinced. Nobody knew what to do with her.'

Except Bob Mercer, that is. He'd been keeping a close eye on her progress and once a month he'd met with Kate to see how things were going. EMI had paid for Kate to buy some basic recording equipment to use at the flat so she could keep a record of any new songs. 'The idea of grooming her was not to change her,' explains Mercer. 'It was to prevent her from changing, to bring out what we could see was in there.' Kate had become quite frustrated at times and wanted to plough ahead with some real recording sessions, but Mercer counselled her against rushing anything. 'About eighteen months after the whole thing started, she came to see me in my apartment next door to Abbey Road,' he says. 'She played me two or three songs, then she started dancing right there in my front room, showing me how she wanted to present the song and, for me, that was the transforming moment. This was presumably the stuff she'd learned for her lessons, but it was the fact that she now had the courage to perform in front of me like that. I knew she was ready. Within a couple of weeks, we had her in the studios. I didn't want to miss anything.'

Chapter Five

The Chords Start Telling Me Something

London, 1977

'You get ideas for songs from all sorts of situations. I just start playing the piano and the chords start telling me something. Lyrics for me just seem to go with the tune, very much hand in hand. Some lyrics take a long time to come, others just come out, like, diarrhoea.'

KATE BUSH

KATE BUSH HAD ARRIVED at the studio and was clearly nervous. Eager and hyper at the thought of her first real studio session, this was the culmination of years of preparation. This was what she'd always wanted to do and now, at the age of not quite 19, she was ready to go. After some initial introductions to the band that had been assembled and some basic chitchat, she sat down at the cavernous studio's piano. After clearing her throat, she played her way through a handful of songs. The session players were mesmerised by what they were hearing and Bush immediately grew in confidence as she became lost in her music. She ran through the songs to teach them to the band and then they got down to business. Her debut album was under way.

★   ★   ★

The year 1977 has gone done as a culturally pivotal year in twentieth-century English history. It provided the last real out-pouring of love for the royal family, which came during the Queen's Silver Jubilee celebrations marking 25 years on the throne. Good old-fashioned street parties crisscrossed the nation and Union Flag bunting was one of the year's biggest-selling items. Against this backdrop, and perhaps because of it, the punk music scene burst into the mainstream consciousness. While most people were celebrating the monarchy, the Sex Pistols hired a boat to sail down the Thames while they defiantly sang their anti-anthem 'God Save the Queen'. It wasn't surprising that, after the country's outpouring of love for the Queen, the band were arrested as soon as the boat came to shore.

'I think an interesting thing's happening in the music scene at the moment from the beginning of this year, especially in England,' said Bush at the time. 'It was purely because of punk. It was a very quick dynamic thing that happened and I think its purpose was in order to bring new things out of it. We now have a sort of thing called New Wave, which has come from punk, but it's not like punk at all. It's rich in interesting lyrics, completely different attitude towards music. There are very interesting lyrics that are based a lot more on reality than a lot of things that have gone before. I think that's the trouble with a lot of music that was happening: things were becoming purely romantic bubblegum. Just talking about boy-meets-girl.'

How Bush felt her debut album would fit in with the musical maelstrom of the times is anyone's guess. The chances are that she didn't care and just ploughed her own furrow regardless of what was going on around her. She'd just turned 19 – and had started seeing Del Palmer – and her songs, while not being 'romantic bubblegum', did tend to be closer to boy-meets-girl than the Sex Pistols' catalogue did.

Bush's romantic relationship with Palmer would be one of the worst-kept secrets in music for the best part of a decade. It was reported that Palmer was initially viewed with suspicion by the Bush family, who as ever were very protective of Kate, especially when they moved in together just as Kate's career was about to take off.

While Kate was honing many of the skills that she'd need in the following years, EMI, and especially Bob Mercer, were also using the time wisely to prepare for the moment when Kate would be ready to enter the studio to record an album for the first time. He spoke with many producers but eventually went back to Andrew Powell, who was deemed the most appropriate and sympathetic to Kate's music and position. The label was also keen to have an experienced set of studio musicians to complement Kate and bring out her best in the studio.

The sessions were planned at AIR studios and Jon Kelly was chosen to engineer alongside Powell. The large Studio Two was pencilled in for the main recordings and Studio One would be used for the string sections, because it was large enough to comfortably house dozens of musicians.

Kelly had earned his stripes working alongside Geoff Emerick at AIR while working on albums by Robin Trowe and Gallagher and Lyle. He'd also learned a lot in a short space of time by recording radio jingles. These traditionally gave a trainee engineer a solid grounding, since they would encompass many different styles of recording and a wide array of musical genres, and require fast turnaround times. All of these were attributes that would come in handy for a career in the world of rock and pop.

Andrew Powell was given the triple tasks of sitting down with Kate to decide which songs to record, to assemble a band to play on the album and to produce/arrange it as well. 'It was very difficult,' he says of the song selection process. 'There were several songs that were obviously very good that didn't end up on the first album. One or two of them were used on the second album.'

For the session band he fell back on tried and trusted players whom he'd worked with before. The KT Bush band was thus superseded by the nucleus of Ian Bairnson on guitar, David Paton on bass, Stuart Elliott on drums and Duncan Mackay on keyboards. Bairnson and Paton came from Pilot and Elliott and Mackay from Cockney Rebel.

Pilot were Scottish contemporaries of the Bay City Rollers (Paton was in an early incarnation of that group), and they had released a dozen singles between 1974 and 1977, 'January' and 'Magic' being the two most famous, reaching Numbers 1 and 11 in the UK charts respectively. The twin waves of punk and disco, added to some poor management decisions, conspired to wash away any chance that Pilot had in the late 1970s and by the time of Kate Bush's debut Bairnson and Paton were held as consummate session players instead.

Steve Harley and Cockney Rebel had formed in 1973 during the height of glam, but only after bringing Alan Parsons in as producer did they make any impact on the UK charts. 'Judy Teen' made Number 4 in 1974 and their most famous song, 'Make Me Smile', topped the charts the following year.

Ian Bairnson explains that EMI had grown to trust the session work of himself and David Paton and that they were regarded as 'proper musicians'. This was especially true after they had worked with the Alan Parsons Project and built up an impressive list of session credits.

The musicians were unaware of Kate's songs before arriving at the studio for the first day of the sessions. This was also the first time they had met her. Both she and her music had an immediate effect on them. 'We found the songs to be very well written and Kate's style had enormous range,' says Bairnson. 'We personally loved the music and her voice, but no one can predict the public reaction to something that different.'

'It's easy to say now, that I knew she was going to have a great deal of success, but that's how I saw it,' adds David Paton. 'She

just played and performed excellent music.' The players' introduction to the music on the first day came when Kate sat down
at the piano and played a few of the songs to them for the first
time in AIR's Studio Two. The band soon worked out their own
parts and on the very first day they had recorded the basic tracks
for 'Moving', 'L'Amour Looks Something Like You' and 'Wuthering
Heights'. The album would take only seven weeks in total.

It wasn't just Kate Bush who was learning quickly as the sessions
progressed. Jon Kelly also had to pick things up quickly. He later
admitted that he'd being feeling insecure going into the session
but that Andrew Powell was the perfect foil to bring him along.
'I give full credit to Andrew and the great musicians, who were
very supportive, while Kate herself was just fantastic,' recalls Kelly.
'Looking back, she was incredible and such an inspiration, even
though when she first walked in I probably thought she was just
another new artist. Her openness, her enthusiasm, her obvious
talent. I remember finishing that first day, having recording two or
three backing tracks, and thinking, "My God, that's it. I've peaked!"'

The musicians were given a fairly free rein to come up with
their own parts to each song. This was partly because of Bush's
inexperience, which meant she wasn't confident enough to tell
the experienced session players exactly what to do, and partly
because Powell had enough confidence in them to let them work
out their own parts. 'Kate was already an accomplished piano
player and singer,' says Bairnson. 'As she ran through each song,
we would use our own instinct to form parts that would complement both the song and each other, not overplaying or showing
off. The songs would quickly develop and the flexibility of
everyone playing together meant that the dynamics and movement
within each song could come through. We definitely worked as a
team and it felt like a natural band. We – David, Stuart and myself
– always had a lot of banter and jokes going on. Kate really enjoyed
that, too, as it kept the atmosphere happy and sharp. It also kept
her nerves at bay.'

The laid-back atmosphere undoubtedly helped ease Bush into the swing of things and right from the off she settled into studio life. 'Kate had the same attitude as us and we all got on with the work with great enthusiasm,' says David Paton. 'We all wanted to do our best. Kate could talk to any one of us as easily as we could talk to one another.'

Bush would play through a song before the basic band track was recorded and Powell provided the players with a chord sheet as a reference for them to play along with. 'I can't read a note of music,' admits Ian Bairnson. 'The songs were colourful and it was just a case of each musician choosing a vibe and a part for his own instrument. Put simply, I didn't always play chords: it could be arpeggios or small answering lines or block harmonies.'

Powell and Kelly would man the control room while the band made passes of each song. At the end of each take Kelly would talk through his comments on that particular attempt and they would run through it again if necessary. 'They kept the vibe going with various [Monty] Pythonesque comments via the talkback,' laughs Bairnson. 'Andrew is a fine arranger and kept check on all things musical, and Jon would check and advise on the sounds we used.'

In this genial atmosphere the sessions progressed quickly and easily. Generally the band would assemble around midday and work for six or seven hours. They'd break for a meal, then return and work well into the early hours, sometimes until three or four in the morning. 'There comes a point where your ears go and you're too tired to think up an imaginative part,' says David Paton. 'There's no point starting another song when you can't give it your best.'

Bush seemed to have unbridled energy and enthusiasm, though. Even when she wasn't actively involved in a stage of the process she'd also be in the studio or the control room trying to sponge up as much knowledge as possible. Her active input was restricted to her piano playing and vocals but she paid keen attention to everything else and was a quick learner.

Once the band tracks and vocals were complete the overdubs were conducted with 30-year-old composer and master percussionist Morris Pert coming in to help out. Pert had done extensive work for the BBC and he spent a whole day adding his percussion skills to numerous songs on the Bush album. On 'Wuthering Heights' he played crotals, which are similar to disc-shaped glockenspiels, and on 'Room for the Life' he added the strangely named 'boo bams'.

After the recording in both of AIR's main studios, the mixing was moved to Studio Three, where a brand-new Neve console was at the service of Powell and Kelly. Kelly spent the first weekend of mixing working on 'L'Amour Looks Something Like You' and 'Moving'. He was ready to finish for the night at about 11 o'clock on the Sunday evening when Powell arrived to inform him that EMI wanted a playback of three songs on Monday morning and Kelly world have to stay and mix another track, which had to be 'Wuthering Heights'. 'We started that mix at around midnight,' recalls Kelly. 'Kate was there the whole time, encouraging us. She was the shining light of the entire sessions. You couldn't deny her anything. So, we got on with the job, and we finished at about five or six that morning. It was a fairly straightforward mix.'

The Kick Inside opened with 'Moving', which in turn opened (and closed) with the weird and wonderful sounds of whales 'singing' to each other. Bush had specifically wanted to open her album this way. This mid-tempo opener allows a gentle entry into the world of Kate Bush. She flexes her vocal range in front of the tight band arrangement. The electric piano is played by Duncan Mackay rather than Kate. As the whale singing closes the first track, it overlaps into 'Saxophone Song', which had been recorded back in 1975 with a completely different set of musicians and when Kate was just 17. Her vocal presentation is quite different with less of the vocal gymnastics and more of a 'straight' performance.

'Strange Phenomena' opens with more electric piano (this time played by Andrew Powell). The subject matter is coincidence but the first verse concerns menstruation ('Every girl knows about the punctual blues'). 'Maybe you're listening to the radio and a certain thing will come up, you go outside and it will happen again,' explains Bush. 'It's just how similar things seem to attract together. Like the saying "Birds of a feather flock together" and how these things do happen to us all the time. Just strange coincidences that we're only occasionally aware of. And maybe you'll think how strange that is, but it happens all the time.' This enhanced her early reputation as some kind of mystic.

Bush wanted 'Kite' to be her Bob Marley song and the verses are certainly semi-reggae, but the chorus takes the song back to more of a classic-rock feel. As with many of the songs on the album, the band were free to improvise on this track. 'Most of it would be up to the individual musician to come up with a good piano line or bass line,' says David Paton. 'I'm thinking of "Kite", where the chords were written but the bass part came out of my head.'

'The Man with the Child in His Eyes' doesn't list the musicians in the liner notes, but this is another song from the 1975 session and would later be released as a single in 1978.

Side One of the debut album ended with what is still Kate Bush's most famous song – 'Wuthering Heights'. Musically, the track is both beautiful and haunting, right from the opening notes. The slow, measured piano chords (doubled with Andrew Powell's chiming celeste) build tension before the vocal gains momentum up to the first chorus, which bursts open with Bush's octave-running vocals. 'I think it is a great track and a style which flew in the face of everything else which was around at the time,' says Ian Bairnson. 'We kept looking at each other thinking, "This is so different but interesting – it will either do really well, or bomb." I don't think there would have been any half-measures in Kate's success, but the Number One spot was a great bonus.'

The skeleton backing track was recorded 'live' in the studio with all musicians playing together: Bush playing a Bosendorfer grand piano, Stuart Elliott on drums, Andrew Powell on bass and Ian Bairnson on an acoustic guitar.

'I can't remember doing any editing on Kate's sessions,' says Jon Kelly. 'I can remember "Wuthering Heights" being a performance-y type song. Stuart was a brilliant drummer – he absolutely adored Kate's songs – and the all-round enthusiasm and will to play well on those sessions was just fantastic. They were great musicians, and everything they did was of a very high standard.'

Overdubs included usual bassist David Paton playing a 12-string acoustic guitar and Bairnson's original acoustic guitar work being double-tracked. The string section (eight first violins, six second violins, six violas and six cellos) and three French horns were recorded in what Join Kelly described as a 'huge room, twice as big as the live area in Studio Two. It could accommodate between 60 to 70 musicians, and had high ceilings and a lovely, bright sound. Everything sounded great in there.'

Kate rerecorded her vocal late one night when the musicians weren't around. Jon Kelly recalls the effort she put into every take that she did. 'In the case of "Wuthering Heights", she was imitating this witch, the mad lady from the Yorkshire Moors, and she was very theatrical about it,' he says. 'She was such a mesmerising performer, she threw her heart and soul into every-thing she did that it was difficult to ever fault her or say, "You could do better".'

The final addition would be Ian Bairnson's guitar solo, which would wind its way over and around the instrumental fade-out of the song. 'For purely "guitarist reasons", I disliked the tone for many years,' reveals Bairnson. 'I prefer my Les Paul [guitar] to sound harder and have more kick, like it usually does on records, but I got over it and am now quite happy with that guitar solo. By the way, there was a much better solo at the end of "James and the Cold Gun" but it wasn't used because of the running time of the album. Maybe one day they will remix that track for CD and include the long outro.'

The solo was actually ad-libbed to some extent when Jon Kelly in the mixing room heard something he liked. 'I remember that while setting up my guitar sound for the solo, I got a note to feed back to the amplifier,' recalls Ian Bairnson. 'When we realised that it was the same note Kate ended her vocal, Jon Kelly, shouted, "Go for it. I'll fade you into the track!" And that's what happened. As Kate sang her long ending note, Jon faded in my guitar holding the same note and I launched into the solo. It was entirely seat-of-the-pants stuff!'

'James and the Cold Gun' is the rockiest song on the album, inspired by the stories of the James Gang, the outlaws who terrorised the American west in the late 1800s. Ian Bairnson's guitar swoops and soars around the simple piano motif provided by Kate.

'Feel It' is the first of two overtly sexual songs, this time about a one-night stand, with Bush openly singing about her sexual longing. Such a 'difficult' topic is presented as a simple piano ballad with only Bush performing on the track. The not-so-physical 'Oh To Be In Love' is sandwiched between the two sexual tracks and concerns the morning after a one-night stand as the singer longs for love and a relationship. But then the lusty 'L'Amour Looks Something Like You' seems to take the singer back on the overt trail. 'It's not such an open thing for women to fantasise about the male body,' Kate said at the time. 'A lot of women, if they see a male pin-up, they think it's funny. I can't understand that. I think the male body is absolutely beautiful.'

The second side of the album ends with a strong trio of songs. 'Them Heavy People' drifts close to reggae at times (like 'Kite') and indirectly talks of the people who have helped her. Mentions of 'Gurdjieff' and 'Jesu' are obvious (and hint at her brothers' influence) but the song most likely also concerns her dance, mime and vocal teachers as well as David Gilmour, whom she thanks on the liner notes for 'rolling the ball' in the beginning – which is the opening line of the song. 'Room For The Life' is a gentle woman's call to arms and a celebration of pregnancy – 'there's room for a life in your womb'.

Ending the album is 'The Kick Inside' and, though musically gentle, it's lyrically very powerful, because it addresses brother-and-sister incest. When the sister becomes pregnant she commits suicide and this song is her suicide note to the brother. Quite a way to go out on your debut album! 'That's inspired by an old traditional song called "Lucy Wan",' Bush explains. 'It's about a young girl and her brother, who fall desperately in love. It's an incredibly taboo thing. She becomes pregnant by her brother and it's completely against all morals. She doesn't want him to be hurt, she doesn't want her family to be ashamed or disgusted, so she kills herself. She says to her brother, "Don't worry. I'm doing it for you."'

In some quarters this album is seen as too twee and dated, but a close listening reveals a real awakening of a strong songwriter. Bush isn't afraid to tackle what were then even more taboo subjects than they are today: incest, one-night stands, period pains and sex from a woman's perspective. No one else was doing this at the time and few have done it since, but it did open the door for female writers to pen more serious songs.

'It's not mainstream, but it's not weird,' says Ian Bairnson. 'Kate has many voices and some of her backing vocals are extra-ordinary. The lead vocals range from quirky to very warm, but always emotive and believable, like a good storyteller. I think the work we did supported her songs and her performance very well.' Indeed musically the album is often more effective at its most simple. Unlike the mountains of overdubs that would characterise her later work the album was recorded relatively quickly. 'After some screens had been strategically placed, there wasn't too much effort expended on attaining separation when the band was playing,' says John Kelly. 'We weren't as precious about that sort of thing back then. The piano wasn't all that far from the drums, yet it really wasn't an issue. For us, the performance was the thing.'

The music business has a lot more to it than simply recording an album and then releasing it to the public. Any illusions about this that Kate Bush and her family may have had were soon dispelled. But, as with each previous step of her tentative career, she received some good advice and everything was done in a well-thought-out and considered manner. Within the first year after releasing her album she would set up her own management and publishing company (more on that later), and she would also run into a wall concerning which track would be her debut single.

In her own mind the choice of a lead-off single was obvious: it had to be 'Wuthering Heights'. EMI, however, had other ideas and wanted 'James and the Cold Gun'. Discussion on the matter started in September.

'It felt like a mission,' she says. 'Even before I'd had a record out I had a tremendous sense of conviction that my instincts were right. There could be no other way. I remember sitting in an office at EMI with some very important people who were saying that "James and the Cold Gun" should be the first single. For me this was just totally wrong. How could it possibly be anything other than "Wuthering Heights"? But they were going, "You don't understand the market."'

'My secretary said Kate was very upset and she wanted to see me,' recalls Bob Mercer. 'She sat down and she said she wanted "Wuthering Heights" to be the first single. I said, "You and I are very close – we should tell the truth to one another. Well, I don't come down to the studio and tell you how to do your job and you're not going to come in here and tell me how to do mine." She burst into tears. I couldn't deal with that. I said, "Frankly, I don't think there are any hits on the album, so I'll put 'Wuthering Heights' out. It will hit a wall and then you'll understand what I'm talking about."'

'So we went on saying the same things to one another for a few more minutes,' counters Bush. 'I was being politely insistent. I usually am in an argument. I'm not good at expressing anger.

That's still hard for me. Then a guy called Terry Walker, another executive, came in with some papers in his hands and put them on the desk. He looked around, saw me and said, "Oh, hi, Kate, loved the album! 'Wuthering Heights' definitely the first single, eh?" And he walked out again. If he hadn't come in at that moment, well, I don't know what would have happened. It was so well timed, it was almost as if I'd paid the guy to do it. They obviously thought of me as just a strong-willed girl, but they trusted his opinion.'

The first battle won, Bush prepared for her first single to receive a November 1977 release. Bush later said that delays over the artwork caused a postponement and things were put back to early 1978. The album's artwork was worked out from one of Kate's own concepts, which she had developed with Del Palmer. She appears quite small on the front and is hanging from a large kite in front of a massive yellow and orange eyeball. The Oriental-styled lettering was perhaps a strange choice, since no other Oriental influence is noticeable on the album. 'I think it went a bit over the top, actually,' she said later. 'We had the kite, and, as there's a song on the album by that name, and as the kite is traditionally Oriental, we painted the dragon on. But I think the lettering was just a bit too much. No matter. On the whole I was surprised at the amount of control I actually had with the album production.'

Certain voices at EMI made clear their unhappiness about the design of the album cover, which they felt failed to show who Kate really was. The picture of her was quite small and the artwork made it seem as if she were Japanese. The powers that be wanted to give her a more focused publicity campaign to push the album and so put together a group consisting of John Bagnall from EMI's new-artist support department, advertising agency Cream and respected photographer Gered Mankowitz.

Mankowitz had made his name while documenting the Rolling Stones' 1965 North American tour. Since then he'd worked with

Marianne Faithfull, Jimi Hendrix, Traffic, Slade, Suzi Quatro and Elton John. It was correctly thought that he would be capable of providing an iconic image to spearhead the forthcoming EMI press campaign. Having been given some background information on Bush, Mankowitz decided he wanted to pursue an image of her that captured the dance side of her character. So, when she arrived at his Great Windmill Street studio in Soho, he suggested that he take photos of her in a leotard.

'I could see that dancing was very important to her,' Mankowitz told Q magazine. 'That gave me the idea of putting her into dancer's work clothes, a leotard, woollen leggings. A couple of days later, I met her and she was wearing thigh-length suede boots and incredibly tight jeans, which really confirmed that her body image was very important to her. I gave her a selection of dancer's clothes and she chose the ones she liked.'

After two hours of hair and makeup preparation, the shoot began and, after a short break for lunch, it continued through the afternoon. 'When she came out of the dressing room, she looked stunning,' recalls Mankowitz. 'So I tired to keep the shots very simple: just Kate against a photo studio canvas background. In the end I cropped the portrait to keep her bosom in the picture, which didn't seem at all inappropriate and she was thrilled with the way she looked.' The shoot comprised shots of Bush in a pink and a green leotard and all the films were handed over to EMI for their perusal. The final choice of a close-up that showed Bush's nipples was bound to create some attention and it became her enduring image and an icon of the late 1970s. The posters that followed became the bestsellers of the year.

'I suppose the poster is reasonably sexy just because you can see my tits,' said Bush. 'But I think the vibes from the face are there.' EMI loved the results of the session and used them every-where. Putting them on the fronts of buses was the marketing masterstroke, though. Stories began circulating that buses were being delayed because passengers in the queues at bus stops were gawping at Kate's photo rather than hurrying onto the bus and that accidents had been caused because the picture was distracting to other drivers. 'It was done with Kate's full approval,' says Bob Mercer. 'We knew it was quite subtly sexual, but that was the first point when her family became a bit protective.'

EMI in their haste to test the water had already sent out promotional copies of the 'Wuthering Heights' single to several radio stations. Despite requests to hold back from playing them until after Christmas, the stations played it anyway.

At London's Capital Radio, producer Eddie Puma played it to DJ Tony Myatt and they both agreed they had to put it on air right away, because it was so original. Night owls in the London area were thus the first members of the public to hear the song on *The Late Show* in November 1977. Soon afterwards Piccadilly Radio in Manchester followed suit and the single spread across independent stations around the UK like wildfire. When Radio 1 (which then still enjoyed a modicum of influence over the record-buying public) also put it on its playlist, the buzz really began to grow. By the time the single actually hit the shop shelves, almost everyone had already heard it.

The next twelve months would prove to be the most taxing period in Kate Bush's life. Physically it would be exhausting, mentally it would be tough and emotionally she would be torn between the open public examination of her personality and the complete privacy she so longed for. The most difficult thing she would have to deal with would be the lack of control of her own destiny. So far she and her family had been able to control things at a steady pace, allowing her to blossom in her own time. Now, though, things were about to happen so quickly that she'd be swept well along the path to superstardom before she'd have a chance to pause for breath and take in what was happening to her world. And that was just the beginning.

Chapter Six

Channel It Into Your Writing

London, Germany, Japan, France, 1978

'I'm nineteen, but so what? I've had experiences too. A lot of my songs are about my own traumas. The best time for writing is when you're going though a heavy time. You have an enormous amount of energy. The best way to deal with it is not to bottle it up or take it out on someone else, but to channel it into your writing.'

KATE BUSH

N A CIRCUS TENT the scene was quite surreal. Hundreds, if not thousands, of holiday makers sheltering from the elements were watching the male half of Abba introduce the next artist on the variety act's bill. Dressed in shiny blue shirts and white trousers, Benny and Bjorn looked like a strangely attired, low-rent comedy duo and they had material to match. 'Whose dancing is amazing?' they asked. 'Whose looks are amazing? Whose voice is amazing? Is it a bird? Is it a plane? Is it a tree? No, it's a bush. Kate Bush!'

Given the opportunity to lip-synch to the massed crowd and the TV audience of millions, she was not going to pass up the chance. The mime to 'Wow' was heartfelt and impressive. As every film director would say, she was really 'making love to the camera' with every nuance and suggestive glance. After the show, though, there was little time for schmoozing with the celebrities backstage: it was straight off to the next promotional assignment. Welcome to the world of Kate Bush, Britain's newest superstar.

★   ★   ★

The year 1978 started fairly quietly. Making the news were the usual kinds of items that had made the news for the previous few years and would continue to do so until the present day. The Egyptian President Sadat and US President Carter were discussing Middle East security problems; Geoff Boycott became the England cricket captain and Sweden banned aerosol sprays because of newly discovered degradation of the ozone layer. Musically the album charts were topped by a K-Tel compilation, *Disco Fever*, while the Sex Pistols (*Never Mind the Bollocks, Here's the Sex Pistols*), Rod Stewart (*Footloose & Fancy Free*) and Donna Summer (*Greatest Hits*) all had albums in the diverse UK Top 10.

EMI held an international sales conference in January at which Kate was asked to sing from her forthcoming album. This was the basis of her introduction to the sales teams that would be pushing her music to stores, and they had previously heard very little from her. She went down a storm and the reps enthusiastically returned to their patches ready to do battle on her behalf.

On the 20th of the month 'Wuthering Heights' was finally released, three months after the originally planned date. The buzz that had been building since November gathered momentum. From the early days of the single's release people were raising their eyebrows and asking, 'What is this song?' 'Whose voice is that?' The tabloid press soon started looking for an angle, and they didn't need to go far to get one: a sweet 19-year-old girl with a screeching voice and 'weird-looking' video. A girl who sang about a Victorian novel and who shared the birthday of the book's writer (Emily Brontë was born on 30 July 1818). When journalists also realised that Brontë had written only a solitary novel before her death at the age of 30 from TB, the comparisons of a one-hit wonder were soon bandied about with respect to Bush. She was in danger of immediately being filed away as a novelty act.

Not surprisingly, the reactions in the music press were mixed. After all, this was a song that defied categorisation and was unlike anything that most people had ever heard before. It was certainly out of step with the rest of the charts. *Melody Maker* offered that she sounded like 'a cross between Linda Lewis and Macbeth's three witches', though they generally liked the song. The *Record Mirror* didn't like it and called it 'B-o-r-i-n-g'. One complaint from listeners was that they couldn't understand what Kate was actually singing in the song. Radio DJ Jonathan King took the extreme step of playing the song line by line and reading out the words from a lyric sheet to satisfy people's curiosity.

Despite all of the early airplay dating back to the previous November, the song's ascent of the singles chart was a slow one. It took a couple of weeks for it to creep into the Top 50 at the modest Number 42 slot. Kate, meanwhile, began what would be a gruelling promotional tour. EMI somehow wangled a spot for her on the German TV show *Scene 78*, also known as *Bio's Bahnhof*, on WDR. She was going to sing her debut single and the album track, 'Kite'. Both songs would be performed live, so the KT Bush Band were resurrected for the trip. One problem was that the drummer of choice didn't have a work permit and couldn't leave the country. At very short notice they needed a replacement.

'At the time "Wuthering Heights" was released, I was actually still living at my parents' place in Chiswick, as the music industry wasn't as lucrative as I first thought and I was still struggling to establish myself,' recalls Charlie Morgan. 'I remember one morning, I had just heard "Wuthering Heights" on the radio, and the phone rang. It was Del [Palmer] on the phone. They were leaving for Germany to do a TV show the next morning. I was not doing anything that week, so I said yes. And so my first professional engagement with Kate was *Bio's Bahnhof*!'

Before flying to Cologne, Morgan received a copy of the not-yet-released album via courier and set about learning some of the songs. 'I listened to the songs and made some notes, before leaving home early the next morning,' he recalls. 'The first time we played the tunes was during camera run-through on the afternoon before the show! Kate was more nervous than I was, I think. But we acquitted ourselves well.'

The show, filmed in Cologne, was a live TV chat show with the musical sections performed in what was a disused railway sidings. First up was 'Kite', which the band played live, dressed in all-white suits to contrast with Kate's bright red dress. Then, for 'Wuthering Heights', she mimed alone to a pre-recorded track in front of a bizarre backdrop depicting an erupting volcano! The mainly middle-aged German studio audience were clearly bemused and didn't quite know what to make of it all but they offered a polite round of applause at the end of the song. 'A fascinating experience,' says Bush of her first TV appearance. '[They had] all these black rolling hills with lightning bolts painted in, and in the middle of it all this dirty great big volcano. They did their best. Obviously they're not that familiar with the scenery on the Yorkshire moors.'

Back in the UK, as the single continued its slow rise, Kate was asked to appear on the prestigious BBC TV show *Top of the Pops*. Over the next few weeks she filmed several versions of the song for the programme, which also screened the song's promotional video, directed by Keith Macmillan. On her *Top of the Pops* debut, following Blondie's 'Denis', Bush was instantly thrust into millions of living rooms around the country. She immediately gave schoolgirls a role model to follow if they wanted a pop career and gave boys a UK sex symbol to follow instead of the aforementioned Debbie Harry.

'For me, that's what this type of exposure did: it made me feel like I'd lost pieces of myself,' says Bush. 'That I'd become a public person, and the private person, and that's who I really am, was actually getting very frightened and lost.

'My first *Top of the Pops* I didn't want to do. I was terrified. Seeing the video afterwards was like watching myself die. That was when things started getting very difficult for me because until then it had all been very creative work, writing, recording, learning to dance. [Now] I was talking to press, talking to television, and I couldn't express myself easily. I was up against a different beast.'

Those who knew her closely perhaps found it hard to equate the family-oriented, girl-next-door type to the picturesque, gyrating sex symbol with the freakishly high-pitched voice and weird videos. On top of the Mankowitz photographs the video to 'Wuthering Heights' pushed her further into the sex-object category and no doubt detracted from her initial efforts to be considered a serious artist. Looking back at Bush's early videos with over a quarter of a century's perspective, one can readily see how the press at the time found it easy to label her as the wide-eyed witch of pop music. One of the promotional clips opens with her rising out of what resembled a low-lying cemetery fog wearing a white dress and looking like a version of Elsa Lanchester in *Bride of Frankenstein*, especially when she puts her arms out in front of herself and strides forward through the fog. Bush certainly wanted to exhibit her dance training in the clip but numerous cartwheels, exaggerated mimes of the song's lyric and flailing arm movements mainly detracted from the overall performance of the song. It is unfair of course to hold music videos of the 1970s up against those of today, and the special effects (multiple Kates and echoey-ghosts) seem harshly dated, a bit like an outtake from Tom Baker-era *Doctor Who*. Despite these drawbacks, the video was highly influential and launched a thousand Gothic lookalikes in pale makeup and long, white dresses at rock clubs up and down the country for years to come – especially as the dress was see-through when lit from behind, as it was in the video. The alternate video of Kate cavorting around a field in a red dress was not nearly so iconic, though it was screened extensively in Australia.

In the aftermath of the *Top of the Pops* exposure, Kate continued the rounds of TV shows (the BBC show *Saturday Night at the Mill* and the kids' show *Magpie*, where she looked extra-Gothic with her white face and lots of candles). *The Kick Inside* was finally released on 17 February 1978 and media coverage intensified. Such a young, seemingly naïve and beautiful girl clearly caught the public's imagination. She did her own thing, steadfastly refusing to follow trends while making career decisions that some saw as inspired and others as crazy. Either way she did things her own way and for the most part was loved for it.

All of the hype culminated in 'Wuthering Heights' becoming the UK's Number 1 single on 7 March. The single knocked super group Abba's 'Take a Chance on Me' from the Number 1 spot. Kate Bush was only 19 at the time. 'Wuthering Heights' would sell a quarter of a million copies in the UK and be certified 'Silver' (today, sales of just 100,000 qualify for 'Gold' status, highlighting the importance of the singles charts then compared with now). Having an English singer at Number 1 clearly pleased the mainstream press. WUTHERING WONDERFUL!, exclaimed the *Daily Express*.

Kate's instant celebrity was confirmed when EMI put on a champagne celebration for her in Paris and there were reports that she'd splashed out on an expensive grand piano with her earnings. This was unlikely, because she would probably not have seen any of the money at such an early stage. The single remained at Number 1 in the UK for four weeks while riding high all over Europe and charting well in South Africa, Australia and beyond.

Both the specialist music press and the mainstream papers found *The Kick Inside* hard to pin down. Much of the album was unlike anything they'd heard before and reference points were few and far between. She was compared, usually erroneously, to everyone from Patti Smith to Lynsey DePaul. 'Kate's extraordinary vocals skate in and out, over and above. Reference points are tricky,' said the *Melody Maker*. The *Record Mirror* seemed unsure of whether the album was good or not. It claimed the album was quite 'normal' but also that 'the sophistication is tremendous for anyone, incredible for a teenager'. *Sounds* was scathing though, complaining that the album contained 'some of the worst lyrics ever . . . with the most irritatingly yelping voice since Robert Plant'. Well he'd done OK, hadn't he?

Many reviewers missed, or chose to ignore, the fact that many supposedly taboo subjects were being addressed by this petite teenage girl. Incest ('The Kick Inside') and period pains ('Strange Phenomena') were mentioned and she would continue to cover these topics on her next album.

With her face plastered on posters across the country alongside adverts for the year's big movies, such as *Close Encounters of the Third Kind*, she became an instant household name. Every publication and radio and TV show wanted to speak to her, and she found her self undertaking a crash course in giving interviews. One minute it would be with a local newspaper, the next she'd be chatting to a serious BBC radio presenter. She was referred to as the 'little girl lost in the huge plush armchair' in the *Record Mirror*. Her overuse of words such as 'amazing', 'wow' and 'gosh' in her interviews reinforced the stereotype of her still being a little girl in a woman's body. The press seemed to forget that she was still only 19, and a few weeks before no one had even heard of her. Later the *Sunday Telegraph* would describe her as a 'curious mixture of naïveté and sophistication'. It was this inability to pigeonhole her that made her interesting right from the beginning.

'Being regarded as a sex object just gets in the way most of the time unless it's relevant to the role I'm playing in the song,' she said. 'Guys get it, of course, but only those that seem to ask for it. Girls seem to get it whether they want to be regarded in that way or not. To overplay it is wrong. It can't possibly last.'

Of course it did last, but she managed to control it better as her career progressed. She rebelled against any form of sexual conditioning and commented, 'Little girls are still given dolls and prams to play with. So many of them grow up thinking their one function in life is to have a baby.' While Kate had been given fluffy rabbits and a Wendy house to play in, her being around two elder brothers and their friends obviously helped her confidence and she was comfortable dealing with men from a very early age despite attending the all-girls school.

In April, as *The Kick Inside* peaked at Number 3 in the UK album chart, Kate was off to Europe again. This time she appeared on TV shows in Holland (where she performed a handful of songs in a Gothic theme park and had a commemorative headstone laid in her honour!), France and West Germany.

'The Man with the Child in His Eyes' was released as the second UK single at the end of May and made the UK Top 10 by July. Many listeners were taken aback and surprised that this was the singer who had screeched her way through 'Wuthering Heights'. This is exactly what Bush had wanted. She was scared of being cast aside as a novelty act, so this 'serious' track was a welcome respite from the 'Wuthering Heights' hype. The video, another Keith Macmillan effort, did nothing to dampen the image of Bush as a doe-eyed little girl, though. She was dressed in a figure-hugging, all-in-one, sparkly suit that made it look as if she were practically naked. It was an outfit that Britney Spears would virtually copy for her 'Toxic' video 26 years later. For this softly focused film, Bush writhed around on the floor waving her arms a little bit, and again there were multiple Kates on view at some points. Three on this occasion. The single would reach Number 6 in the UK chart.

In the name of publicity she would fly off at a moment's notice. One such occasion was to appear on Italian TV. 'To me it was bizarre,' she says. 'Up in the morning, over to Verona, I think it was, and walk out on this stage. I'm facing the cameras and a few hundred people who I assume are the audience. Then the stage and the whole set starts to rotate and I realise that it's a huge circular stadium and out front there are thousands and thousands of people. I've never seen so many people in my life! Anyway, I mimed "Wuthering Heights", bowed, and flew off home again.'

Such was the price of fame. Bush didn't want to completely sell herself out but she felt she had to promote herself to a certain extent in order to get her music to as wide an audience as possible. It was along these lines that she agreed to participate in the Seventh Tokyo Song Festival. 'Moving' had been released as a single in the Far East and her appearance there helped it go to Number 1. The song festival was actually a competition (won by the American soul legend Al Green) and Kate took second place in front of a TV audience of more than 30 million and a live crowd of around 11,000. A BBC TV crew followed her around as she tried to take in some Japanese culture in between a long line of interviews and promotional appearances.

In midsummer she managed to get away from the spotlight for a while before resurfacing in September. Before the end of the year, Bush made one of the more astute moves of her career when she set up her own management company. Through Dave Gilmour, she had hired Pink Floyd's lawyer, Bernard Sheridan, to set up the company. He also arranged for Bob Mercer to renegotiate Bush's contract with EMI and she gained ownership of all her own recordings from 1980. The new setup, which included holding companies and covered everything from song publishing to promotional photographs to fan club newsletters, was named Novercia and in true Bush tradition was a real family affair. Novercia was now in the position to license Kate's works back to EMI as a third party. The directors of Novercia were listed on the Companies Register at Companies House as Patrick Bush, John Carder Bush, Catherine Bush, Robert John Bush and Hannah Patricia Bush.

Behind the scenes during Kate's first year in the limelight there had been numerous power struggles as both the label and the family jostled to guide Kate's career – while she wanted to guide it herself. An unnamed EMI executive was quoted as saying, 'It was often very frustrating for professionals in the business that a doctor and an elder brother were making decisions on your decisions when they were not really qualified to do so.'

John Bush had initially been placed as Kate's management representative but EMI installed Peter Lyster Todd in that position, though he had to undergo an informal interview over dinner with the Bush family. 'He has worked more on the theatrical side of entertainment than music,' said Kate at the time. 'I like that. I think most managers are crooks, greedy and nonmusical, and that mixing with other music managers is contagious. I think Peter will be amazing.' Quite how Kate knew that 'most managers are crooks, greedy and nonmusical' is uncertain and probably goes no further than a general stereotype that she'd been warned against by her brothers and father.

Todd certainly had his work cut out. The family wanted to keep a tight rein on how Kate was presented in public, especially after their unhappiness over the initial Mankowitz photographs. But at some point she was also allowed to be photographed in Holland with what looks like a stuffed dolphin. The resultant pictures are ridiculous, to say the least. She was also snapped in some fairly tame 'bondage' outfits. These were bought by the *Record Mirror* and Peter Todd tried unsuccessfully to pay them off so that they wouldn't go ahead and print them. Whether these photos had been taken while Kate was still under family management is unclear, but the relationship between Todd and his client lasted only a matter of months before he was out of the door.

Hilary Walker, who had been head of EMI's international promotions, took Todd's place. 'I see myself as her personal assistant but we're really more like close friends,' said Walker. 'We discuss offers and what to wear for shows. My role is to act as buffer between Kate and the outside world. I take all enquiries and offers for her work and we discuss them as friends, but the decisions are always hers.'

'Because my family were involved I was with people I could trust,' Bush added. 'I feel quite worried about mentioning the companies' names [though they were printed everywhere]. When you're doing interviews you have to be almost like a security guard sometimes.' This paranoia would spread through her entire career.

On 5 September Bush appeared on the *Ask Aspel* children's TV chat show. This programme was hosted by Michael Aspel, the long-running BBC radio and TV presenter. It came as something of a surprise when she debuted a brand-new song, 'Kashka From Baghdad'. She wanted to debut another new song, 'The Warm Room', but the BBC found its sexual content too close to the bone for a children's show, so instead she sang the aforementioned new song, which was about two gay lovers, which the BBC were OK with. For a children's show, many of the questions were quite enlightening, and it was the first public indication that she had been working on new material. Of course, she was also asked the usual questions about her biggest hit. 'Because of the subject matter and the fact that I'm playing Cathy and that she was a spirit and it needed some kind of ethereal effect, and it seemed to be the best way to do it, to get a high register,' she explained. When asked about her newfound wealth, she told the young viewers that she'd invested it back in a home studio: 'We built a studio at my parents' place, so we've actually got a demo studio and we can use it for recording and helping the band and all sorts of things. Pretty useful.'

The announcement on this show that Kate had used some of the money to construct a home studio was news to most people. It was also newsworthy that she'd recorded a second album over the summer. Singles from her debut were still in the charts and she was recording the next album already! From late spring members of the KT Bush Band had been working at the farm, which, despite the ring of protection surrounding Kate, had been publicly revealed as her home base. From the earliest days Hannah Bush would answer the door to fans who would just arrive unannounced at the farm to leave gifts and items to be autographed by Kate, but on the whole it didn't cause many problems.

Drummer Charlie Morgan had been called upon to play on the demos for the new album and enjoyed the fact that it was all well away from London's bustling music industry. For him the farm was a welcome sanctuary and he was happy to be involved in setting up a studio there for Kate. 'We spent several weeks during that time ripping out walls in the barn,' he recalls. 'After that, we soundproofed it all, put in double glazing and wired up the main studio components. Some of this was done while Kate was away in Japan, promoting *The Kick*. By the time she returned, we had a fully functional eight-track demo studio.'

Once the studio was operational Kate and the KT Bush band immediately put it to use on a whole set of new songs that she'd prepared very quickly. These informal sessions were laid back but long. 'When she's in the studio, Kate loses track of time, and so some days could be very long,' says Charlie Morgan. 'Whenever I drove down to the farm, I knew to block out the entire day, and not to expect to get home until the wee hours of the morning! Often we would order delivery – Indian was our favourite – and sit there in the control room or outside if the weather allowed. I have vivid memories of Kate's mother interrupting us on occasion, with tea and biscuits. I would always try to take a few minutes to pop into the house and say hello to whoever was there.

'I have very happy memories of it all,' Morgan continues. 'The band were all working towards a common goal. We had stars in our eyes. I was totally bedazzled by her, incidentally. But, as fellow Leos, we were prone to frequent disagreements about how songs should go, which songs to choose and so on. Something the family were a bit bemused by!'

By the summer of 1978 Kate was the UK's fastest-selling female artist as well as having Number 1 singles in Australia, Belgium and New Zealand. She was given just four weeks to come up with new material and she had to delve back into her demo tapes to provide enough material for an album after penning three new tunes in the allotted time.

On the recommendation of David Gilmour, who'd recorded his eponymous debut album there earlier in 1978, Kate decided to record her second album at SuperBear Studios near Nice in France. Already, at this very early juncture in her career, Bush felt rushed and hemmed in by record company requests and demands. Though she had new material and had made the demo recordings at the new home studio, she felt that she was being unduly rushed into finishing the follow-up album.

'I felt very squashed in by the lack of time, and that's what I don't like, especially if it's concerning something as important for me as my songs are,' she said in 1978. 'I was getting a bit worried about labels from that last album. Everything being soft, airy-fairy. That was great for the time, but it's not really what I want to do now, or what I want to do, say, in the next year. I guess I want to get basically heavier in the sound sense . . . and I think that's on the way, which makes me really happy. If you can get away with it and keep changing, great. I think it should be done because in that way you'll always have people chasing after you trying to find out what you're doing. And, anyway, if you know what's coming next, what's the point? If I really wanted to, I guess I could write a song that would be so similar to "Wuthering Heights". But I don't. What's the point? I'd rather write a song that was really different, that I liked, although it might not get anywhere.'

The album that would become *Lionheart* was demoed in its entirety at the farm before Kate left for France in July 1978. Once she was there, though, the atmosphere changed with the presence of producer Andrew Powell. It soon became apparent that Powell wanted to use the backing band who had recorded Kate's first album, namely Stuart Elliott, David Paton and Ian Bairnson. Bush wanted 'her' band to record the album and a power struggle ensued over who would record it.

The KT Bush Band had already recorded six tracks at the French studio before Powell and EMI won the day and a change in personnel was made. 'Andrew Powell reined us in quite severely,' recalls Charlie Morgan. 'There was a little bit of subterfuge going on, too. He had signed a deal to produce the second album, and naturally wanted his boys to do it. Kate was adamant that she wanted us to do the album. So we were caught in the middle of a tug-of-war.'

The final indignity was when Morgan and the others left France only to meet their replacements arriving at Nice airport to take their places!

'Andrew had a meeting with Kate, and threw out all but two of the backing tracks – "Kashka", and "Wow",' Morgan explains. 'With hindsight, I totally understand what was going on, and the motivation of the individuals involved, but at the time we were gutted. Imagine, our dreams of actually being heavily involved in a major international success story were dashed. In the end, Andrew Powell's band used the demos as reference points, and recut most of the album. It's interesting to note that we never held a grudge against these guys. We understood what had happened, even then. Kate was really upset about it all, of course.'

It took a while but the wounds eventually healed with time and Morgan later made friends with all involved. He and David Paton toured and recorded with Elton John from 1985 to 1988; he played with Ian Bairnson for Beverly Craven between 1990 and 1992; and he later collaborated on the rhythm tracks for many of Kate's recordings with Stuart Elliott. 'I even made my peace with Andrew Powell many years later when, as a session drummer, I turned up on sessions for a *Classic Rock* album that he was producing,' says Morgan. 'We were able to put it all down to "water under the bridge". Somehow I knew it wasn't because he disliked me or my playing. Such are the politics of the music business.'

The setting of the French studios couldn't have been better. It was a residential facility with its own chef, two cascading swimming pools and a games room. Having been kitted out by Eastlake Audio, the studio was decorated in the style of the times – a lot of fake rock and cork tiling. The control room was not huge, but the studio itself had a number of isolation booths, with a drum booth off to one side. The entire studio was under the main part of the house, which was on a hillside, so you entered the house itself from the middle floor with bedrooms upstairs and the studio below. It was nestled in the Alps with glorious sunshine and mountain air, making it sometimes difficult for Kate and the band to concentrate fully on the job at hand. Ten weeks later, though, there were 12 songs completed and 10 were chosen for the album *Lionheart*.

'It was an amazing experience,' said Bush at the time. 'It's the first time I've ever recorded out of the country and the environment was really quite phenomenal. It was just so beautiful, it was so unlike anything I'd seen for a long while. The fact that it was so beautiful, you couldn't help but keep drifting off to the sun out there. Because the vibes and the weather and everyone around was just so good, you didn't feel like you were working.'

'It started out great and just got better and better,' says David Paton. 'I even bought the albums I didn't play on. I loved the music and the playing. Kate is a real musicians' musician.' Just as the Bush entourage moved out, Queen arrived to record their album *Jazz*.

Lionheart was important for Bush in several ways. First she'd had to provide a new album at short notice to maintain her momentum and keep EMI happy and she'd managed it under copious amounts of pressure. She had also kept an eye, and ear, on a future tour. She had wanted the new material to fit in with her advanced vision of what that tour would be: a totally theatrical experience unlike the usual rock and pop shows of her contemporaries. So the music had to be able to blend with that of *The Kick Inside* and be able to be reproduced in a live setting. She managed all of this and soon the public would get the chance to share her vision of a unique live performance.

Chapter Seven

We Are Ruled By Everything Around Us

UK, European tour, 1978–79

'I think there's a lot in astrology. I think it's a very ancient, well mathematically planned-out thing that a lot of people boo-hoo. And I think it's very unfair, because there's a lot of very strong, scientific knowledge in there. I think it's been commercialised a lot, which is why people become so cynical. But I think the fact that people are born at a certain time, on a certain day, with stars in certain positions is bound to have some effect on that person because we are ruled by everything around us.'

KATE BUSH

STOCKHOLM, SWEDEN. A strange blue-green light from the back of the set illuminates a large net curtain that separates the crowd from the stage. The weird sounds of whale songs twist and turn their way from the sound system and then the mysterious form of someone slowly flapping their arms is exaggerated to larger-than-life proportions in a giant shadow across the curtain. The net is slowly pulled to one side revealing Kate Bush at the bottom of a ramp. She's wearing a microphone headset, which allows her to move freely around the stage as the band, now visible on either side of the ramp at the back of the set, open with 'Moving'. Bush's voice sounds pretty good, even though this is her 16th show in three weeks and she's been suffering with a sore throat that almost meant the cancellation of this date. The fans present, while enjoying the show, don't realise that this will be the only time they will have the chance to see a Kate Bush concert.

★   ★   ★

Lionheart in many ways is quite different from *The Kick Inside*, but the oft-cited speculation that Bush's writing had matured is wide of the mark. First, no one would mature that quickly: it was only a few months between album releases. Second, as discussed earlier, the first album had many mature songs on it already. Third, many of the songs on *Lionheart* predate some of those on *The Kick Inside*. Bush had been given only a few weeks to write more songs, so she'd naturally gone back to her older material as well to provide an album's worth.

Estimates vary, but it's likely that less than half of the album was actually written in 1978. 'There were quite a few old songs that I managed to get the time to rewrite,' she says. 'It's a much lighter level of work when you rewrite a song because the basic inspiration is there – you just perfect upon it and that's great. And there are about four new songs so they all came together – it was great. In fact, we ended up with more then we needed again, which is fantastic.'

Kate, knowing she'd be touring after the release of *Lionheart*, wanted to make sure that many of the songs were very dramatic. She managed to achieve the combined sound of a movie score and a musical revue. Her voice sounds more controlled and this is evident from the opening 'Symphony In Blue', which was inspired by/borrows from Erik Satie's *Gymnopédie No. 2*, though it isn't credited in the liner notes. Musically this track could have

A rare opportunity to see the Bush family relaxing at the farm.
From left to right: Mother Hannah, brother Paddy, Kate and brother John.

A very slim-looking Kate faces the
press around the time of her first
album in 1978.

Kate at an early photo shoot in her favourite knee–high boots.

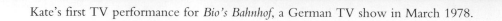

Kate's first TV performance for *Bio's Bahnhof*, a German TV show in March 1978.

Kate flies high on her only tour in 1979.
Here she is helped by Stewart Avon Arnold and Gary Hurst.

Kate pre-empts Britney Spears' see-through costume from her 'Toxic' video on this *Saturday Night Live* performance in December 1978.

Kid Jensen (*right*) is on hand as Kate starts picking up industry awards. In February 1980 at the Café Royal, Kate received an award for Top Female Singer of 1979 during the British Rock and Pop Awards.

Kate helps promote the International Year of the Child in November 1979. Here she is snapped with The Who's Pete Townshend (*left of Kate*) and Thin Lizzy's Phil Linott (*behind Kate*).

Kate as the gun-slinging space-cowgirl on tour, 1979.

Kate blows away another victim during 'James and the Cold Gun', on the Tour of Life.

Kate and Bob Geldof celebrate each winning an award for Best Single in 1979.

Kate's awards came from all manner of publications and institutions. Here she collects an NME award from friend and collaborator Rowan Atkinson.

Hounds of Love put Kate firmly back on the TV and in the public eye.

been the theme tune to a TV show, but the lyric 'The more I think about sex/the better it gets' would put paid to any chance of that.

'In Search of Peter Pan', a child's take on growing old, reinforces the theatrical nature of the album with its use of 'When You Wish Upon a Star' (which is credited) from Walt Disney's *Pinocchio*. 'A young innocent mind can be just controlled, manipulated, and they don't necessarily want it to happen that way,' says Bush. 'It's really just a song about that.'

By Track 3, 'Wow', if you weren't already picking up the theatrical vibes from the record then this track rammed them home and left no doubt. From the opening line about being all alone on the stage, through the lines about the homosexual actor not making it to *The Sweeney*, it's all about show business. This is one of the tracks that were retained on the album from the original KT Bush band recordings and features Charlie Morgan, Del Palmer and Brian Bath. Bush said she had wanted to sit down and write a 'spacey Pink Floyd kind of song'. She certainly achieved that feel for the song. 'I really enjoyed recording "Wow",' she said. 'I'm very, very pleased with my vocal performance on that, because we did it a few times, and, although it was all in tune and it was OK, there was just something missing. And we went back and did it again and it just happened, and I'm really pleased with that – it was very satisfying.'

Her flippant description of redoing the vocals is at odds with Andrew Powell's memories of the sessions. 'Kate got far more self-critical, wanting to sing things again and again,' he says. 'For "Wow" she did a very musical guide vocal, but she sang it maybe four or five times an hour, ten hours a day for a week. At times one would try to convince her that her performance was great, but if she was really unhappy she had to have the chance to do it again. She was optimistic every time.'

Kate also managed to use many of the words that she'd been ridiculed for overusing in her early interviews – 'amazing', 'wow', 'fantastic', etc. The sublime structure and composition of the song made it one of her most complete works to date.

'Don't Push Your Foot on the Heartbrake' was meant to be a Patti Smith type of song, and, though Bush failed to match the animal intensity of Smith's most dramatic works, it did rock along quite nicely.

'Oh England, My Lionheart' demonstrated an abrupt change of pace to end Side One. The song is given an almost medieval arrangement with just simple piano, recorders, harpsichord and a delightful Bush vocal. When taken separately, the lyrical references seem to be very stereotyped English icons (London Bridge, Shakespeare, the Thames, the Tower), but she pulls it off with a kind of perverse longing that doesn't turn to treacle.

In later years Bush seemed to regret the song's inclusion, but it's the real centrepiece of the album. 'It makes me just want to die,' she said more than a decade later. 'There's just something about that time. It's such an old song. I haven't heard it for so long. Must have been on tour in 1979. England, yeah, I am happiest here. We're a funny race. We give each other such a hard time, don't you think? One thing we take very, very seriously is this whole business of taking the piss, the whole stuff about irony. I think there's a real integrity about us under all the layers and our sense of humour is so strong.'

'Fullhouse' seems to be a song about someone struggling with inner demons and a split personality and is followed by 'In the Warm Room', which was yet another open song about sex, but this time written from a man's perspective. 'I'm always getting accused of being a feminist,' said Bush. 'Really I do write a lot of my songs for men, actually. There are so many songs for women about wonderful men that come up and chat you up when you're in the disco and I thought it would be nice to write a song for men about this amazing female. And I think that I am probably female-oriented with my songs because I'm a female and have very female emotions but I do try to aim a lot of the psychology, if you like, at men.'

'Kashka From Baghdad' tells the enigmatic, but melodic, tale of two gay lovers who hide away in their little house. This was another song that had been inspired by something that Bush had seen on television. '[It] came from a very strange American detective series that I caught a couple of years ago, and there was a musical theme that they kept putting in. And they had an old house, in this particular thing, and it was just a very moody, pretty awful serious thing. And it just inspired the idea of this old house somewhere in Canada or America with two people in it that no one knew anything about. And, being a small town, everybody wanted to know what everybody what else was up to. And these particular people in this house had a very private thing happening.'

Bush displays a well-rounded vocal in the verse and then double tracks her voice to mesh with the backing vocals as the song rises up. Paddy Bush gets down to some serious work on this track, playing strumento da porco, mandocello and pan pipes, and singing harmony vocals.

'Coffee Homeground' returns to the theatrical feel of Side One and musically could be the accompaniment to a circus juggler or high-wire walker. The story within the lyric is actually a dark tale of murder, poison and intrigue. The inspiration for the story came from a strange source. 'It was inspired directly from a cab driver that I met who was in fact a bit nutty,' she laughs. 'It's just a song about someone who thinks they're being poisoned by another person. They think that there's belladonna in their tea and that, whenever they offer them something to eat, it's got poison in it.'

The album closed with a really dramatic piano opening to 'Hammer Horror', the name of the famous British horror film company that churned out numerous grisly tales in the 1960s and 1970s. The televisual inspiration came not from the English studio that she took for the song's title, though, but from seeing James Cagney playing the part of Lon Chaney playing the Hunchback of Notre Dame in the 1957 film *Man of a Thousand Faces*.

The album's cover again featured Kate in an unusual pose. This time she was pictured crawling over a wooden box in a lion outfit to fit the title. The lion's head sits on the floor beside her. Gered Mankowitz took control of the art direction and photography based on a design by Richard Gray, which in turn was based on an idea from John Bush.

'We wanted to get across a vibe within me of a lion,' says Kate. 'For the front cover it basically comes from an idea that my brother had, which was an attic setting with me in a lion suit, so it's slightly comical, but just a really nice vibe on the front that would take away the heavy, crusader, English vibe, because *Lionheart* is always associated with Richard the Lionheart. And I think it's a word that could become more readily used, it's such a beautiful word. It's kind of like "hero", and "hero" is a very clichéd word now. It's used in so many songs.'

Mankowitz built the set for the shot at his studio and spent a day photographing Kate in the lion suit. The sessions were exhaustive and Kate's ever-creative impulses and urges could prove tiring for collaborators who were constantly trying to keep up with her flood of ideas. When they were finally happy that a suitable shot had been achieved in the lion suit, they moved on to some close-up portraits the next day.

Other photographs in the package, the portraits again taken by Mankowitz, showcased Kate in her big-hair phase, backlit and topless as far as the camera can tell. The idea was to have what amounted to two front covers for the album, though one just happened to be on the back. 'I'll always play up for photographers,' she adds. 'I can't stand there looking miserable – it'll get printed anyway. To cope I have to play the complete loon. I do have to keep my face in the papers, you know. I need the publicity.' Mankowitz shot Bush on four or five occasions and provided the cover image for this book.

Once mixing for the album was complete Kate had been put straight back onto the promotional treadmill. This time she flew to Australia and then went on to New Zealand. TV appearances were planned and such was the haste of her schedule she would be up until the early hours devising dance routines for the new songs that she'd be performing on TV the very next day.

In November the album was officially launched in Holland, for some unknown reason, and Kate continued her promotional tour into Germany and France. 'Hammer Horror' became the first single from the album but peaked at Number 44. The video was rarely shown on TV and the song failed to catch the imagination of radio stations. Had her bubble burst? Had she been pushed down people's throats too much in her first year? Any worries about an overkill of celebrity were dispelled when Bush won both Best Female Vocalist and Brightest Hope of 1978 at the *Melody Maker* awards dinner in early 1979.

Releasing two albums in the same calendar year, having undergone a baptism of fire in the press and been halfway around the world on promotional trips, Kate Bush seemed to be something of a superwoman. Interviewers were as keen as ever to see what she had to say (and comment on what she was wearing) though she downplayed being part of any celebrity circuit. 'I don't like showbiz,' she told BBC Radio 1. 'I very rarely go to parties. If I go to one of these dos it's because people have been good to make the effort to vote for me and I think I should say, "Thank you" rather than, "I can't be bothered to come, send it round."'

Melody Maker opined, 'The enigma that is Kate Bush, it confuses us all.' But what was this enigma, if it wasn't just a persona concocted by the press? So she was young but didn't like going to show-business parties. Did that make her some enigmatic mystic? No.

In December she made another long-distance trip, this time to North America. After the relative indifference to her first Stateside visit earlier in the year, this time she was invited to sing live on NBC's *Saturday Night Live*. While one Kate Bush website blusters that 'nothing remotely like it has ever been seen on American television before', this is just the type of overblown generalisation that such websites are often critical of when the press makes such wild comments about Bush!

It was actually an unusual performance. First, she wore her sparkly body suit as she sat cross-legged on top of a grand piano to sing 'The Man with the Child in His Eyes' and followed it up with 'Them Heavy People', wearing her fedora and a raincoat. The show, on this occasion hosted by Eric Idle, always received a massive viewing audience but she needed to make much more of a sustained effort to break into mainstream America. She returned home still something of an unknown in the USA.

Solo female artists were still in a very small minority in an industry that was very much run and directed by men. Donna Summer, Diana Ross, Olivia Newton-John and Elkie Brooks, all of whom had had recent hit albums, couldn't claim to have as much artistic input into their material as Bush did into hers. She was already setting new standards.

Kate Bush would soon be the subject of a handful of quickly written, poorly produced books that showed little more than a willingness to cash in and concentrate on as much 'controversy' (real or otherwise), gossip and conjecture as possible. Either much of the gossip was true or the Bushes couldn't be bothered to contest it (which seems unlikely), since the books weren't withdrawn and in future years at least one would be revamped and reissued.

Official merchandising was also still blooming. In the first year it's estimated that more than 30,000 posters of Kate were sold for bedroom walls around the country. Sales of drawing pins and wallpaper-ruining Blu-Tack must also have risen. But, as the Bush camp celebrated a fantastic first year in the public eye, the country as a whole was dipping into the depths of depression and disillusionment. The so-called 'winter of discontent' was taking a grip on the country as Prime Minister Jim Callaghan fell out of touch with the mood of the country. When asked about the growing unrest among unions he replied that there was no need for concern, giving rise to the famous newspaper headlines of CRISIS? WHAT CRISIS? Things went from bad to worse as unemployment rose and strikes became commonplace. The dead weren't being buried and dustbins were piling up on city streets as the collections were cancelled. By May 1979 Callaghan was gone as Margaret Thatcher swept to power. But, away from the social strife around the country, Kate Bush continued to collect more accolades that were thrust her way.

Bush had managed to survive a hectic first year and learned a lot along the way. In a year that had seen her at her most out of control and exposed, she now knew that she didn't like gimmicky promotion, didn't really like interviews, didn't often like reviewers and really didn't like being out of control. So slowly the family dragged it all back in.

On 2 January 1979, during a particularly cold spell, there were comings and goings at the East Wickham Farm. Rather than stragglers from a New Year's party, the assembly was very much business-oriented. The first ever Kate Bush tour was being discussed. Production designer David Jackson was present to talk through preliminary ideas for a tour that would take several months of hard work to bring to fruition. This was not going to be a typical band on tour, just playing their songs and then moving on to the next town. This was going to be a full-on theatrical production with a large supporting cast. Besides Kate and a seven-man band, she would employ two female backing vocalists, two male dancers and a mime/magician.

EMI were reluctant to put their full financial backing behind such an unusual venture, so Bush ploughed a large amount of her own earnings back into the project. 'I don't see myself as being a publicist for myself,' she said, 'but a publicist for my music.'

Some of the band selections were no-brainers for Kate. She was helping to foot the bill, so she would decide who played what and when. Del Palmer would play bass, Paddy Bush would add his weird array of ancient and ethnic instruments and background vocals while Brian Bath would reprise his role from the early KT Bush band days and play guitar. Auditions were held for the other band places that were up for grabs. Alan Murphy had to audition for the tour with other guitarists before, a few weeks later, getting the call that they wanted him to join. Other successful auditioners were drummer Preston Heyman, who would also go on to play on Kate's next two albums; Ben Barson (brother of Madness keyboard player Mike), who was added as a synthesiser and acoustic guitar player; and the versatile Kevin McAlea, who got the call to play piano, keyboards, saxophone and guitar. Thirty-year-old McAlea was one of the most experienced musicians on the tour and played a self-built keyboard during the shows. He hadn't heard much of Kate's music aside from the omnipresent 'Wuthering Heights', so when he was invited to visit the farm he had to be shown the songs there and then before he could play through them with the band. He obviously impressed, but it took a few weeks before he was officially invited to participate.

The backing vocalists were Liz Pearson and Glenys Groves, and Stewart Avon Arnold and Gary Hurst would be Kate's dance partners. Both dancers had performed on numerous TV appearances with Kate while Hurst had also sung harmonies and improved her fitness levels with his with dance-practice routines.

The dance routines were to be a cornerstone of the show. By the autumn of 1978 Kate had been attracting so many onlookers to her dance classes at the Dance Centre that she had had to move to the London Contemporary Dance Group under the tutelage of Anthony Van Laast. 'Anthony helped me to extend myself,' she says. 'Like any good teacher he pushes you. So many teachers never want you to be as good as they are, but not Anthony. He was so encouraging.' Van Laast was therefore the main choreographer for the tour.

The final member of the onstage crew was the illusionist and mime Simon Drake. He was a fairly novel addition to a rock and pop tour, though he had worked previously with Camel and Lene

Lovich. He had been working on prototype effects for a possible tour for over a year and when he was told it was definitely going ahead he ran through some ideas with Kate, Paddy and Del Palmer.

From early dance rehearsals in Covent Garden and band practice at Woodwharf Studios in Greenwich, the whole production moved to a soundstage at Shepperton Film Studios, where the dancers and musicians worked together for the first time. The show would be running for about two and a half hours a night and Kate would be physically exerting herself throughout, so her physical training was heavily regimented. 'It's something that you do have to work up to because the movement takes up a great deal of breath and the singing takes up as much, so you literally need twice as much breath to handle it,' she says.

'It was really just working up to it, stamina. When I began the first few weeks of my training I would never have been able to do that whole show. I'd have just passed out in the middle of it. It's really just the adjustment and also adrenalin, because once you're up there you just cannot do anything wrong. If you do you're letting down all the people that have come to see you. And that's what performing is all about: you have to die for them. And so I think I'd probably hold my breath and die rather than show it. It does become a performance once you're up there, and things tighten up that you never thought would.'

As usual the latest Kate Bush project was a family affair. Hannah would visit the rehearsals, helping out with tea and biscuits for the weary artists. John Bush's wife Judith provided vegetarian meals to keep the 30-strong entourage going on a daily basis and Paddy Bush was, of course, already part of the stage production.

After several weeks of 14-hours-a-day rehearsing they moved to London's Rainbow Theatre for some full dress rehearsals, which continued for a further two weeks. Bush was trying to keep details of the show as a closely guarded surprise until the opening night, but of course the popular press tried their best to get a sneak preview for their readers. One photographer did manage to breach security but he was caught and had his film confiscated. One of the innovations that were worked on during the rehearsals was Kate's use of a cordless microphone headset. Although it's now famous for being used by Madonna, Bush pioneered the idea from an experiment with a humble coat hanger. She really needed the freedom to be able to dance and move freely around the stage during the tour and so this necessity pushed forward the invention.

Before the end of March the whole tour, including some extra dates that were added late on, was sold out. Some members of the newly created official Kate Bush Fan Club were heartbroken when their 'guarantee' of two tickets each to any show of their choice was not upheld by many of the venues and they didn't get to see the tour. The club could only apologise.

To build up excitement for the tour EMI released 'Wow' as the next single from *Lionheart*. The video was premiered on ITV's *The Kenny Everett Video Show* of all places but fell foul of the overly picky BBC censors and a revamped version was shown on *Top of the Pops*, because Bush was too busy with tour rehearsals to appear in person. The video itself was another lip-synched effort, this time on the empty stage, as sung about in the song. Again, multiple Kates appear, this time floating in front of a bank of floodlights.

Finally the time had come to perform the entire show in front of an audience. Before the 'official' tour began the show was booked in for a one-night-only engagement at the Poole Arts Centre in Dorset on 2 April. This abridged warm-up show lasted two hours and was a great success. The cast and crew travelled back to their hotel and they began an impromptu celebration. The 'real' tour was due to start in Liverpool the following evening and everything was perfectly poised.

Back at the Arts Centre a few last-minute checks were being carried out. The equipment had been loaded for the journey north and lighting designer Bill Duffield was having a last look around the stage area to make sure nothing had been left behind. Someone had left an open panel in the flooring and tragically as Duffield crossed the dimly lit stage he tripped and fell 17 feet onto a concrete floor under the stage. He was rushed to hospital and placed on a life-support machine in intensive care. Back at the hotel the party came to an abrupt halt. Understandably everyone was devastated by the news. Then a decision had to be made as to whether or not the tour would continue. The general consensus was that Bill would have wanted them to continue and so they did. A week later he died of his injuries in hospital.

Kate Bush's one and only tour couldn't have been further from a 'normal' tour. At two and a half hours long, only the Grateful Dead or Bruce Springsteen could challenge her stamina. Or that of her audience. The set list was the same each night and there was little or no interaction with the crowd. Large curtains draped the stage, slides and films were shown on large screens, Kate changed costumes virtually every song. The Rose of Lee pub this was not!

Split into three distinct 'acts', the show incorporated panto-mime, dance and magic and had a circus feel to parts of it. Even the programme that was sold at the shows was something special. Housed in an A4-sized folder was a 12-page glossy colour brochure, three colour postcards of Kate, and a letter from fan club director Nicholas Wade. The letter actually explained at which points the audience were allowed to leave their seats and had a suggestion form on the back, which could be deposited at special boxes on the way out.

So, finally after months of preparation and excitement, the lights went down at the Liverpool Empire for the first show of the tour. *Record Mirror* reported,

> This wasn't just a glamorous show or a lavish display of nouveau camp theatrics but the ultimate rock and roll extravaganza complete with an exciting display of props, a well drilled, unob-trusive backing band and a pair of black dancers whose main

mission in life appeared to be hurling amazing Kate from one end of the multi-tiered, strobe-lit stage to the other.

The large gauze curtain captured a large shadow of Kate as she entered the stage via a rear ramp. The whale sounds of 'Moving' coincided with her entrance and waves were projected onto the screens. The opening song was played pretty straight and Kate seemed to be easing into proceedings.

Act One would comprise seven songs from *The Kick Inside* and two completely new numbers. Costume changes would flow thick and fast. 'Saxophone Song', 'Room for the Life' (which sees Simon Drake on stage in a Carmen Miranda outfit complete with fruity headgear), 'Them Heavy People' (with a dance routine virtually identical to the video) and the crowd-pleasing 'The Man with the Child in His Eyes' came before the debut of 'Egypt'. 'L'Amour Looks Something Like You' saw Kate dancing in front of mirror through which the mysterious Mr Drake again appeared. Another new song 'Violin' came next and showed off some of the stranger stage effects. Two human-sized violin costumes flanked Kate while Simon Drake acts as a mad fiddler who plays faster and faster until billows of smoke rise from his instrument. (The words to this song changed during the tour before it was included on Kate's third album, when the lyric used was eventually settled on.) 'The Kick Inside' closed the opening act.

Act Two focused on a change in mood, with five songs from *Lionheart* in this six-song section. The mood that came across was one of sex. 'In the Warm Room' initially had Kate playing solo at the piano but, as the tour unwound, she asked Kevin McAlea to play it for her so she could sing and move around the stage. 'Fullhouse' and 'Strange Phenomena' carried the mood.

Bush was showing great control and poise with her vocals. The band were competent without being flashy. In fact even though they were all assembled around the rear of the stage they were pretty conspicuous by their 'absence'. It was Kate who was defiantly the star of the show. 'Hammer Horror' saw Kate dance a complicated routine similar to the promotional video for the song but she didn't sing it live. A prerecorded track was played (this was explained beforehand), though she didn't try to lip-synch to it. 'Kashka From Baghdad' faded into traffic noises as Stewart Avon Arnold and Gary Hurst entered a blackened stage carrying electric torches as a prelude to 'Don't Push Your Foot on the Heartbrake'. Kate appears as the lights come up slightly to reveal all three in black leather jackets. Kate sings behind a wire-mesh fence as a very urban dance routine ensues with the two male dancers using dustbin lids as props.

The final act comprised a mixture of songs from the first two albums. 'Wow' recreated the dance sequence from its video, though not quite as successfully. For 'Feel It' Kate was back at the grand piano. For 'Symphony In Blue' the musical score was projected onto the piano's lid. 'Kite' was given an elongated instrumental introduction before Kate arrived down the ramp with the dancers, and then 'James and the Cold Gun' brought the house down in a hail of imaginary bullets. Bathed in red and green light, Bush emerged in a black body suit with gold trim and elbow-length gold-coloured gloves with a gun holster and 'Emperor Ming'-styled gold collar to give her the look of a futuristic space cowgirl. Towards the end of the song she toted a rifle and blew away several cast members before celebrating the violence at the top of the ramp. Today, in the age of gangsta, this would be seen as ill-advised at best and wildly irresponsible at worst, but back in the 1970s guns were mostly only seen on TV, not on the high street.

While the encores were staged, there could really be only two songs that she would sing, since she'd already covered just about every song on each of her albums. For 'Oh England, My Lionheart' she donned a flying jacket and a leather pilot's hat to pay tribute to fallen heroes of the past. And the last song of the night had to be 'Wuthering Heights'. In a live setting her most famous song came across as fairly pedestrian, but the crowd loved every second of it and she was given standing ovations across the board.

From Liverpool the tour snaked its way around England and Scotland. The entourage travelled on a specially outfitted bus with what was then considered a state-of-the-art video recorder and cassette deck. The crew would watch old westerns and listen to a diverse selection of music covering Eberhard Weber to Devo. Two nights in Birmingham followed the Liverpool show, then it was south to Oxford, Southampton and Bristol before two shows back up in Manchester.

In between shows she was photographed with Prime Minister James Callaghan, who was about to lose the general election to Margaret Thatcher. Sunderland and Edinburgh followed with a press conference before every show. The first leg of the tour culminated in five nights at the London Palladium. The broadsheets were out in force to report on this cultural phenomenon. 'A dazzling testimony to a remarkable talent,' raved the *Telegraph* while the *Guardian* said that, 'Kate Bush live for the first time was very impressive'.

The European leg of the tour opened in Stockholm on 24 April, but only after a scare over Kate's voice. She was struck down with a sore throat while flying to Sweden and it was touch and go right up to show time whether they'd have to cancel. The combination of good Scandinavian doctors and Kate's following their orders not to talk saved her voice. The show was trimmed down a little, as were the following shows in Copenhagen, Hamburg and Amsterdam, which completed a busy schedule of four shows in six nights. The rest of the tour zigzagged from West Germany to France and back. Kate's parents flew over for the Paris show and then it was back to London for the Bill Duffield tribute show.

As a benefit for Duffield's family Bush played an extra show at the Hammersmith Odeon with Peter Gabriel and Steve Harley. The two singers had joined Bush in Amsterdam to rehearse for the tribute show and they performed a rousing version of the

Beatles' 'Let It Be'. The following night Keith Macmillan shot his live tour film, which was released two years later.

Overall the tour must go down as an artistic success, though it was reported that Bush lost thousands of pounds that she'd pumped into the project from her own funds. As a spectacle it was unique; as a combination of her most beloved art forms it was a triumph; but for some tastes it was too theatrical for a rock and pop show. Pretentious voiceovers and static set lists were a turn-off while the lack of spontaneity and dynamism didn't make for exciting repeated viewings. It seemed to be *too* choreographed. The lack of interaction with the crowd, not even a 'Hello' between songs, suggested an aloofness; and the lack of a theme or narrative connecting the songs rendered the theatrical presentation of them little more than a collection of set pieces that she could have performed on TV's *Wogan*.

Taken individually, the songs were great but as a whole the extravaganza fell flat and didn't really work as an exciting rock show in which you didn't know what was coming next. She reacted to the criticism of aloofness by arguing, 'I really hope people understand why I didn't talk to the audience during the show. It would have been out of place. On stage I'm not me, I'm trying to create a mood and character. I was speaking in so many other ways that words were not really worth their money.'

In August Kate and Jon Kelly went back to the collection of live tapes and worked their way through them to mix the sound-track to a planned tour-video release and a four-song live EP called *On Stage*, which was coming out in September. The EP featured 'Them Heavy People', 'Don't Push Your Foot on the Heartbrake', 'James and the Cold Gun' and 'L'Amour Looks Something Like You'. But Kate wasn't happy with the sound. So, in an act of perverse logic (and hinting at the later obsession with tinkering with her recordings), she went back and rerecorded some of the parts to make them sound more 'live', which surely defeated the whole object of its being a live EP.

The *Live at Hammersmith Odeon* video was eventually released in 1981 to stem the grumblings about there not being a second tour. For those who missed the original shows it was cut down to a disappointing 52 minutes from the original two and a half hours that were performed each night. The most obvious missing songs were those from Act Two, which were a little bit saucy. The 12 songs that were included gave a decent overview of the tour and were linked together by use of some of the projected images used in the actual shows. In lieu of a real tour, it's not surprising that it sold very well indeed.

Kate has got off relatively lightly over the years in terms of escaping a real bashing in the press. She has given plenty of scope to put herself in the firing line, but most times the sense of respect that she commands has saved her from any real critical fallout. In autumn 1979 she did get a bit of a bashing from the *NME*. Danny Baker was given the job of interviewing her, even though he knew little about her music.

With a relatively free and easy run into the end of the year, Kate took the opportunity to appear at a small number of seemingly random events. In November she was invited to sing at the London Symphony Orchestra's 75th-anniversary concert alongside Cliff Richard. Why she was asked is unclear, since she had very little in common with either the organisation or fellow singers Cliff Richard and Labbi Siffre. She did, however, make the actual performance quite special by singing 'Blow Away' in memory of Bill Duffield. She also popped up at the *Melody Maker* awards to collect the Best Female Singer prize. During November she also made a stop at Abbey Road to record a new song for a Christmas single. 'December Will Be Magic Again' was recorded, but they ran out of time to release it, so put it back until Christmas 1980.

Between Christmas and New Year the BBC aired a 45-minute Christmas TV special, which Kate had recorded back in October. Part of the show had been recorded at South London's Nunhead cemetery. The long hours that Kate was willing to work for such a relatively short clip emphasised the work she was willing to put in for her art. The segment preparations for the cemetery sequence had begun with makeup at a folding table in Kate's front room at seven o'clock in the morning. The whole cast and crew then drove to the graveyard, which was a nineteenth-century Gothic masterpiece dedicated to the affluent dead. Here they filmed a sequence for 'The Wedding List'. Further – indoor – parts of the show, which included a duet with Peter Gabriel on Roy Harper's 'Another Day', were filmed at the BBC's Pebble Mill studios in Birmingham. This extravaganza marked the end of a busy year and left Kate with the opportunity to slink out of the public gaze for a while. She wouldn't be taking it easy, though: she already had an eye on her next album.

Chapter Eight

It's All Up To Us

London, 1980

'I think a lot is gonna happen [in the 1980s]. A lot that hasn't happened for maybe thirty, forty years. There's so much building up. And looking at the music business I've never known so many top acts bringing out albums, all of them. And it seemed reflective of how bad a year we'd had. It's almost like all that really bad, negative energy has made all the creative people go, "Right, I'm going to channel it and write it down." And it helps, because if you've got lots of really good music to listen to then it helps you too. You listen to it and think "Yeah, I can channel it too." So it's all up to us, this ten years, it really is. It's up to all the human beings alive, to do what they can, isn't it?'

KATE BUSH

THE FILMING HAD BEEN taking place since early morning and both the cast and crew were cold and tired. As usual on a Kate Bush video set, she could be difficult to please and was hardworking, while expecting the same of everyone else. Her natural enthusiasm was usually enough to carry everyone along, but her single-mindedness and her attention to detail could mean take after take after take. And, at this point, standing in a couple of feet of cold water in the middle of a forest was not something you'd want to spend more time on than was necessary. The cast were all wearing white nuclear-fallout suits and finally Kate agreed that having them completely submerse themselves in the lake, in order to be filmed emerging from the water, was more than one could reasonably expect. So instead they were filmed waist-deep in the water, and later, while they sat around the edge of the lake, the film of a nuclear bomb exploding in reverse was superimposed on the footage. Was this really a Kate Bush video?

★   ★   ★

The 1980s was going to be the decade of the future. It would be all computers, mobile phones, CDs and the Sinclair C5. Science fiction was going to come true and everything was going to be better. Wasn't it? In reality the Soviet Union had just invaded Afghanistan, Reagan would soon become the US president and the Cold War was a chilly as ever.

Musically, punk had died out and disco was slipping away, the New Wave, post-punk bands would soon storm the charts and electronic music would grab a strong foothold over the music scene. But, for now, the first chart of the decade had seven 'Best Of . . .' records and compilations in the Top 10, proving that good new music was hard to find.

During the relative calm of the months since *Lionheart*, Kate had been manoeuvring against the backdrop of two years of success to enable her to make some of her own decisions. She managed to win some key battles about who would play on her third album and where it would be recorded. Eventually she decided to stay in London this time and work at the world-famous Abbey Road studios.

Bush wanted to co-produce the record and Jon Kelly was 'promoted' from engineer to co-produce alongside her. He was also very familiar with Abbey Road, having worked there extensively for the past few years with Geoff Emerick. 'The whole thing was so exciting for me, to actually have control of my baby for the first time,' said Bush. '[It was] something that I have been working for and was very nervous of, too, because when you go in for the first time you really wonder if you are capable – you hope you are. Every time that we tried something and it worked it just made you feel so much braver.'

Bush had come across some new ideas about recording techniques and production that had come from an unlikely source. Just after she started demoing material at Abbey Road's Studio Two in January 1980 she agreed to sing on two songs for Peter Gabriel's solo album *Peter Gabriel*. Both 'Games Without Frontiers' and 'No Self Control' were later released as singles, reaching Numbers 4 and 33 respectively in the UK singles chart. What she found most fascinating about working on these tracks was the way in which Gabriel composed his music using a drum machine and electronic sampler as his main 'instruments'. This of course was completely at odds with Bush's preferred method of using the piano or sometimes a guitar to compose. She would increasingly use samplers, especially the Fairlight CMI, as the decade progressed.

Instead of going in with an album's worth of songs ready to record, the method of writing and demoing in the studio was also a new way of working for Bush, and she spent almost five months at Abbey Road, starting in January 1980. This was not a cheap luxury, because the studio was charging the then expensive fee of £90 per hour, which over a five-month period added up to the princely sum of roughly £100,000 on studio hire alone.

During this period she found the time also to guest on Roy Harper's *Unknown Soldier* album and receive a plethora of new awards. These included being voted Best Female Artist by the *Record Mirror*, the *NME*, *Music Week*, *Sounds* and Capital Radio.

Kate had used the intervening months to write completely new material, having used up most of her early tunes and lyrics over the first two albums. The subject matter was typically edgy, though, and she wasn't afraid to hit out at political themes, too.

The two diverse methods of composing that Kate was employing during this period are highlighted by two very different demos of a brand-new, hook-laden song called 'Babooshka'. In the first demo she put down the basic track with a piano as the only musical accompaniment along with some backing vocals on the chorus. This is how she'd been recording since her earliest home experiments. Then you can also hear the approach of her use of a beatbox click track to give a basic rhythm over which she has recorded the piano and vocals. Both methods are successful in their own way and the song shows great promise at this early stage, even though the vocals are not the final ones used in the released version.

Kate had total control over the musicians employed for the sessions and members of the KT Bush Band played prominent parts on the album, as did her brother Paddy. Partly this was down to his expertise with ancient and forgotten instruments, which he learned to build himself. On the finished album he was credited with a weird range of instruments, including the balalaika, Delius, koto, strumento de porco, banshee and even the 'musical saw'! This is in addition to more mainstream instruments such as the mandolin and sitar. Oh, and he sang back-vocals, too. 'He's always had a great fascination for the beauty of instruments from the past,' says Kate Bush. 'He went to a college where he learned to build early musical instruments and the more he's been getting into it the more he plays.'

Kate says Paddy had always been in and around the recordings but this time she wanted him to input more from his weird and wonderful repertoire. 'I think one of the great things about this album is that it left much more room for people to do things than on the other ones,' she says. 'It was that direction, much more experimental, exploring. And Paddy played a big part with all the instruments exploring little pieces and areas, absolutely invaluable. Very like animation, his instruments. They just put a little bit of red on here and a little bit of green down there and complete it.'

Bush ensured that the long months holed up at Abbey Road were made as comfortable as possible. With family and friends all around, she filled the studios with plants and flowers, held chair-spinning competitions, embarked on late-night high jinx with stolen alcohol and of course lots of chocolate and cigarettes.

With her continued reluctance to undertake another tour, the videos that accompanied her singles took on a greater importance for Kate. These were the only visual way she could communicate directly with her audience now. She was beginning to think of their visual presentation very early in her song-writing process, wanting to translate the theatrical approach that she'd used on her tour into the medium of the three-minute pop video. 'I find it gets easier with most of them to create the visual ideas,' she said at the time. 'Sometimes it's harder. It really does depend on the song, because the song lays down every key move: who you are, what you wear, what colour the set is, you know. It's really the song dictates it all.'

Bush was certainly one of what she referred to as 'the television generation'. She hadn't read a great deal as a child but had spent hours in front of the TV, especially because she was a fan of old films. So she knew the medium she was aiming at very well and she used this 'inside knowledge' to great advantage during the middle of 1980, when the pop video was really something of a novelty. MTV was still 18 months away from being launched and the UK had just three television channels, BBC1, BBC2 and ITV. The best way to get your music on TV was to produce a video that *Top of the Pops* would show to its millions of regular viewers.

Once the sessions for *Never For Ever* were wrapped up there was a surprisingly long wait for its release date, planned for September, and EMI took the unusual step of releasing two advance singles from the album. The first of these, 'Breathing', caused a mini-sociopolitical storm with its images of nuclear war. 'I came up with some chords that sounded to me very dramatic,' says Kate. She's right, as well. The striking opening to the song gives a real sense of doom that pervades the entire track. It is sung from the viewpoint of an unborn baby inside the womb, and depicts the effects of nuclear fallout as they pass through the mother and into the child ('Outside gets inside'). The vocal is tinged with panic through the verse and then it gently lullabies through the chorus as instinct takes over and the baby breathes rhythmically. Comically, a EMI executive who visited the studio while they were working this song thought it was a sexual song and asked what she thought she was doing recording such a pornographic chant ('Out-in, out-in, out-in'), but he only went to prove that many listeners got the wrong impression of what her songs were really about. The contradiction was never more evident than when another EMI rep heard this track for the first time in the studio and was moved to tears.

During the bridge a male voiceover describes the effects of the bomb, the bright flash, the fireball, the mushroom cloud and the different sizes of various bombs.

Keith Macmillan again worked on the video for 'Breathing' and came up with a five-and-a-half-minute film that was described as 'epic', 'ambitious' and 'controversial'. In the early 1980s the subject of nuclear war was a touchy one and for those growing up at the time a nuclear holocaust was seen as a more tangible and terrifying threat than world terrorism is today. The Campaign for Nuclear Disarmament was at its peak and the showing of nuclear explosions on television was carefully thought about before being screened. It wasn't until later in the decade that TV movies such as *The Day After* in the US and *Threads* in the UK stunned the nation and pushed the public's panic levels higher. So the use of nuclear-explosion footage in something so 'flimsy' as a pop video was deemed unnecessary in some quarters.

The video was split into two 'acts'. The first showed Kate acting as the baby in the mother's womb. The 'womb' was created by putting Bush in a plastic bubble with a simulated plastic umbilical cord. For the latter part of the film she and the band members emerge from a lake using coloured lens filters for an eerie twilight effect and wearing fallout suits before the image of the explosion at the end. The womb part of the film caused problems, because filming had to be halted every few minutes so more air could be pumped into it. The outdoors shots were filmed at the site of many vampire movies at Pinewood Studios in Shepperton, Middlesex. The long day was completed with the band being filmed in the cold water before the footage was taken away for the addition of some special effects. The ending of the video is where the trump card is played. The nuclear explosion is shown in reverse to symbolise the opposition to nuclear arms.

The video was partly snubbed by *Top of the Pops* (they would only show the first part of the clip) but she was invited onto the BBC's early-evening current affairs magazine show *Nationwide* to discuss the topic in detail. This was one of the few programmes that agreed to show the explosion sequence but it was in the context of a special show focusing on the debate over nuclear weapons. The programme's introduction showed the public's feelings on the matter in stark detail: 'Well, today many people believe that, with increasing tension in the Middle East, we've never been closer to the prospect of nuclear war. And, with headlines echoing that fear over last few weeks, its not surprising that a singer should produce a song with the same sentiments.'

Bush, of course, hadn't just penned the song to coincide with recent news events, but her longstanding nuclear objections came to the forefront of her thinking. 'I hope that we're not drifting towards war,' she said then. 'But it does concern me tremendously, yes, it does, as one of the one of the human beings on this Earth. I think we should be very concerned about looking after each other [rather] than destroying each other, which we are doing gradually, anyway.' So, while the subject was always of concern to her, it was nonetheless seen as quite a departure from her previous output.

(As an aside, it's worth noting that, in World War One, Kate's grandfather, Joe, had been jailed because of his stance as a conscientious objector.)

The 10th of May saw the inaugural Kate Bush Fan Club convention at the Empire Ballroom, Leicester Square, in London. A slightly disappointing 300 fans attended – perhaps most club members didn't know what to expect. As far as fan club conventions go, those who didn't attend probably missed out on one of the better ones in fan club history. Keith Macmillan's film of the 13 May 1979 concert was given its first public viewing and tracks from the as-yet-unreleased album were played, accompanied by slides of Kate's early life taken by her brother John. To cap it all, Kate herself turned up at the end to say thanks and sign autographs.

While Kate took a break after the convention, the following month saw the release of another advance single. This time 'Babooshka' was chosen, and it created another mini-storm, this time over the provocative outfit that Kate wore in the video. As in the song, Kate portrayed two characters in the video. The first character was garbed all in black with a veil and acted with a double bass. At the chorus the warrior queen 'Babooshka' bursts forth, backlit in her skimpy outfit, showing lots of flesh.

Like 'Breathing', 'Babooshka' opened with some dramatic piano chords, but this was a song that told the story of a wife who took on a new persona to see if she could seduce her husband while disguised as a Russian spirit. This was based on the story 'Sovay Sovay'. 'Sovay' had long been a country and folk singers' standard and Martin Carthy had made a famous version in 1965. The original story told of a 'highway-woman' who tested her husband by trying to steal his wedding ring. He wouldn't give it up, thus unwittingly proving his love to her.

'It was very strange, because, as I was writing this song, the name just came and I couldn't think where I'd got it from,' said Bush. 'I presumed it was from a Russian fairytale – it sounded like the name of a princess or something – and it was so perfect for the music. It had all the right syllables and the right feel, so I kept it in. Many strange coincidences happened after that. I'd turn on the television and there would be Donald Swann singing about 'Babushka'. So I realised that there was actually someone called this and I managed to find in the *Radio Times* a little précis of a programme that was on called *Babushka*. It was an opera that someone had written and Babushka was apparently the lady that the three kings went to see because the star stopped over her house. They presumed that the Lord was in there, and when he wasn't they went on their way. She wanted to go with them to find Jesus and they wouldn't let her come so she spent the rest of her life looking for him. I don't really know where it came from but it worked.'

The single was a slow burner but eventually it reached Number 5 and became her most successful single since 'Wuthering Heights'. Later that summer, John Lennon bought a copy to play to his musicians to show them the kind of sound he wanted for the *Double Fantasy* album, which he was recording. He was shot dead in New York just a few months later. In 1981 Bush bought several Lennon-related items at a rock and pop memorabilia auction at Sotheby's in London.

Never For Ever could be quite a confusing title, but, when explained, it's quite simple. It was Bush's play on the fact that life is transient, death is inevitable, we are 'never for ever' – a theme that she explored on the album with songs such as 'Blow Away', 'The Wedding List', 'Army Dreamers' and 'Breathing'.

'The other two albums were what I would call glossy, and I could understand them saying that,' said Bush at the time. 'I feel this one is the rawest it's been, it's raw in its own context. [I was seen] as this chocolate-box-sweetie little thing who has no reality in there, no meaning of life.' So with this in mind she produced an album that certainly had its darker moments as well as some of the taboos that she had addressed on the first two albums.

One of the pre-release singles, 'Babooshka', opened Kate Bush's third album. The breaking glass that faded 'Babooshka' out led directly into the strange animal that is 'Delius (Song of Summer)': short on words and long on drum machines, weird male vocals and Paddy Bush's sitar. The subject of the song was born Fritz Theodor Albert Delius, the classical composer better known by his anglicised name, Frederick. In his later years he was struck down by illness and, unable to speak properly, he managed to dictate his new compositions from his wheelchair to a string of young musicians who would transcribe them for him. Eventually Eric Fenby (who is name-checked in the song) came to work for the composer and they formed a successful partnership until Delius's death in 1934. 'It was such a beautiful concept,' said Bush. 'This man whose body was almost completely useless and yet inside him all this life and colour and freedom. It was only through Mr Fenby that it could come out. It's such a beautiful story.'

As the robotic beat of 'Delius' faded out, the laid-back sounds of 'Blow Away (For Bill)' took over. The Bill in question was Bill Duffield and the album's theme of death and moving on came into focus for the first time. This song doesn't deal with death as a finality, though. Here the character dies and leaves their body behind, only to have their soul travel around before returning to the body and living again. In the song they meet the a selection of dead performers – Minnie (Ripperton, an American singer, dead from cancer at 31), Moony (Keith Moon), (Sid) Vicious, Buddy Holly, Sandy Denny and Marc Bolan.

'It was really brought on by something, I think it was the *Observer*,' recalls Bush. 'They did an article on all these people who when they'd had cardiac arrests had left their bodies and travelled down a corridor into a room at the end. In the room were all their dead friends that they'd known very well and they were really happy and delighted. Then they'd tell the person that they had to leave and they'd go down the corridor and drop back into their body. So many people have experienced this that there does seem to be some line in it, maybe. It's some kind of defence hysteria, I don't know, but they felt no fear and in fact they really enjoyed it. Most of them have no fear of dying at all. And I thought that a nice idea. What a comfort it was for musicians that worry about their music. They're going to go up into that room and in there there's going to be Jimi Hendrix, Buddy Holly, Minnie Ripperton, all of them just having a great big jam in the sky, and all the musicians will join in with it.'

Bush was still clearly upset over the loss of Duffield and spoke of him in interviews after the album's release. 'In so many ways he made me want to write the song right from the beginning,' she said. 'It was such a tragedy and he was such a beautiful person that it only seemed right that there should be something on the next album for him. It was really tragic that it should have happened and so unnecessary, too. We did the benefit concert for the relatives of Bill, which we hope helped a little, but it's such a helpless situation.'

The stop–start grandeur of 'All We Ever Look For' addresses wants and needs from one generation to the next. 'Because I am a member of a close family they were obviously in my mind a lot,' said Bush. 'It's interesting the things that we do pick up from our parents, the way we look or little scratching habits or something, and obviously the genetic thing must be in there. All the time it's going round in a big circle. We are always looking for something, all of us, just people generally and so often we never get it. We're looking for happiness, we're looking for a little bit of truth from our children, we're looking for God, and so seldom do we find it because we don't really know how to look.'

'Egypt' is a fantastical dream along the Nile with synthesised noodles and effects. 'The Wedding List' is a completely different creature – a bouncy jaunt of a melody through the verse that goes against the grain of the lyric in the chorus: a murder of the groom at his own wedding. As with many of Kate's inspirations, the seeds for this song came from a film, this time it was François Truffaut's 1968 movie *The Bride Wore Black*, which starred Jeanne Moreau. 'Whenever I base something on a book or a film, I don't take a direct copy. I don't steal it,' explains Bush. 'I'll put it through my personal experiences, and in some cases it becomes a very strange mixture of complete fiction and very, very personal fears within me.'

For the track 'Violin' Kate put in a call to an old friend and fiddler, Kevin Burke of the Bothy Band. 'Kevin is a fantastic fiddler,' says Bush. 'He's just wonderful. He's so Irish and so full of the music and he was so perfect for the song.' Burke had been a friend of the Bush family since the 1960s, when he went to school with Paddy Bush, but by 1980 he had moved to Ireland. Paddy called Burke's mother and she passed him over to Ireland. 'Kate was very young when I first heard her,' explains Burke. 'She was writing, playing and singing songs at a very young age, so it wasn't that much of a surprise to hear she had recorded and was very successful.' Burke arrived at AIR studios to overdub his fiddle part but the vague instructions he was given weren't that helpful to him. 'It was a daytime session, the backing track was done already,' recalls Burke. 'The idea was explained to me but, as a part hadn't already been prepared for me, I felt a little out of my depth, as improvising isn't my strong point, especially in a style of music that I wasn't used to. But both her and Paddy were great at "nursing" me through it. I heard the tape of what had been recorded already and Paddy and Kate spoke to me about the atmosphere and mood they were trying to capture.'

Kate wanted Burke to play like a mad fiddler, in the mould of Nero fiddling while Rome burned. 'It was meant to be very fun,' she says. 'Nothing deep and serious, nothing really meaningful, just a play on the fiddle, the things it represents, its madness.' The sonic decorum itself is fairly mad, as it thrashes along at quite a pace with Bush squealing and shrieking along in a way that would have made Siouxsie Sioux proud, and Alan Murphy provides a stinging guitar solo.

'The Infant Kiss' was a tricky song to understand and one that Bush was at pains to explain to the press lest anyone run away with the wrong interpretation of the lyric. Listening to this song would have been helped if you'd seen the film that Kate had in mind when she wrote it: this time it was the 1961 British production of *The Innocents*. In the film Deborah Kerr plays the part of a spinster who takes the position of governess for two orphaned children. She later discovers the grisly secret of what happened to the previous governess and the gardener, the spirits of whom are inside the children!

The way Bush took that story and wove it into the song was explained thus: 'I was imagining that moment of the nanny giving him a little peck goodnight and he gives her a great big adult kiss back. The emotional tearing inside her. There's a psychotic man inside this innocent child, a demon, and that's who this straight woman is feeling attracted to. It's such a horrific, distorted idea it's really quite beautiful. The thing that worries me is the way people have started interpreting that song. Paedophilia. It's not about that at all. It's not the woman actually fancying the young kid. It's the woman being attracted by a man inside the child. It just worries me that there were some people catching onto the idea of there being paedophilia, rather than just a distortion of a situation where there's a perfectly normal, innocent boy with the spirit of a man inside, who's extremely experienced and lusty. The woman can't cope with the distortion. She can see that there's some energy in the child that is not normal, but she can't place it. Yet she has a very pure maternal love for the child, and it's only little things like when she goes to give him a kiss at night, that she realises there is a distortion, and it's really freaking her out.'

'Night Scented Stock' was the almost religious-sounding lyricless vocalisation that neatly linked the ending of 'The Infant Kiss' and the intro to 'Army Dreamers'.

The album closed with two songs that saw Bush delve into the world of political comment. 'I've thought a lot about the political aspect – this is when people label them as political songs,' she explains. 'But it's only because the political motivations move me emotionally. If they hadn't, it wouldn't have gotten to me. It went through the emotional centre. The nuclear situation' – addressed on 'Breathing' – 'is such a real danger, the fact that buttons have been pushed and planes have gone into action. It's something to be scared of, it really is. None of us wants it to happen. We're the innocents. Saying something about it from the heart is not going to change the world or anything, but at least people can think more about it.'

The first of these 'political songs', 'Army Dreamers', concerned British forces stationed in Northern Ireland. Kate was worried about the Irish reaction to the song, so she tried to avoid any direct references to the troubles there. She mentioned the 'BFPO' (British Forces Post Office) in the lyric to give a sense of wider British overseas involvement, though at the time of writing the song there was very little apart from Northern Ireland. She also sang the song with a semi-Irish accent.

'The Irish accent was important because the treatment of the song is very traditional, and the Irish would always use their songs to tell stories – it's the traditional way,' she explains. 'There's something about an Irish accent that's very vulnerable, very poetic, and so by singing it in an Irish accent it comes across in a different way. But the song was meant to cover areas like Germany, especially with the kids that get killed in manoeuvres, not even in action. It doesn't get brought out much, but it happens a lot. I'm not slagging off the army, it's just so sad that there are kids who have no O-levels and nothing to do but become soldiers, and it's not really what they want. That's what frightens me.'

The treatment of the song was one of contradiction with an almost twee, lightweight melody being underscored by the pretty stark words of the lyric. This was the first song that she'd written totally in the studio.

'Breathing' ended the album in dramatic style with doom-laden piano chords just as the closer on *Lionheart* ('Hammer Horror') had. The fade-out refrain of 'we are all going to die' was not perhaps the cheeriest way to start the new decade.

The artwork employed for the sleeves of *Never For Ever* was quite outstanding. Kate herself took the overall credit as art director, while animator and illustrator Nick Price drew the front cover and John Bush took charge of the photography for the back cover. 'The idea [for the front cover] was really mine but the work was totally Nick Price's,' Kate says. 'He really interpreted it as the way he saw it. The idea was that all of us – we are full of all those black and white things, bats and swans; and that the mixture of them is what we are – we aren't just good and we aren't just bad, we are both of them. In my case my black and white thoughts, my emotions, go into my music and on the cover they're coming out from me and going into the album. That is really what we are trying to symbolise, the fact that we are full of many, many things inside us and that they come out at some time, whether it's in anger or whether you channel it into something productive.'

Price is an accomplished illustrator and artist, specialising in children's books. He'd attained an art scholarship from Canford school and worked on many different projects: six murals at Heathrow Airport, 26 episodes of the *Doctor Snuggles* cartoon and three animated films based on Aesop's fables are just some of his credits.

Price was given photographs – taken by John Bush – of Kate standing in front of a large fan to make her dress rise up. Price used this photo session for the cover, which he drew in pencil. Kate then closely followed the progress of the drawing to make sure it was what she wanted. For the back cover she undertook an energetic photo session with John Bush in which she wore a bat costume. The original idea was to have images of bats and doves as the sun set and the moon rose (again to signify the light and dark sides) but in practice the bats worked better alone. As ever, the attention to detail was great and she had her tongue dyed red as part of the self-devised bat makeup. Q magazine's *100 Best Record Covers* special listed the contents of Kate's dress as follows: 'Kate's Cornucopia – Five bats, thirteen birds, seven butterflies, three fish, one anteater, two cats, one dog, one lion, one serpent, one reptile, thirty devils and two "normal people".'

The album was released on 11 September and Kate did a tour of record stores around England and Scotland causing big queues everywhere she went. The accompanying press release documented Kate's ever-expanding list of artistic credits as 'manager, composer, musician, arranger, singer, dancer, producer, live artist, choreographer, designer, session singer and video star'.

Press reaction to *Never For Ever* was generally very favourable. The treatment of adult topics such as war, incest and Northern Ireland were given top billing in reviews and features. Even though other 'taboo' topics had run through each of her albums to date, they just hadn't been as prominent. The adult nature of parts of the album allowed some commentators to reappraise the maturing Bush. Writing in the *Face*, Julie Burchill said, 'I have at last to admire Kate Bush.'

Coverage was widespread as Bush was described as the drama queen of British rock and she made the cover of *Company* alongside headlines such as UNDERSTANDING MISCARRIAGE and SATURDAY NIGHT AND THE SINGLE GIRL.

Peter Powell on Radio 1 asked Kate about her inspiration and again she touched on the influence that television played in her creative process. 'Things people will say, whether they say them on television or to me personally or even things I hear on the radio,' she said. 'It's very much stimulus from other people and just the way I feel about things that I see in other people.'

In the press she sometimes felt stereotyped and was happy to talk to anyone and everyone to expand her sphere of fans. The

Sun and *Company* both carried interviews. 'I think I'm conscious of people doing that [stereotyping] in certain areas, because of the way they've seen me, and I think that's inevitable. I don't blame them. It's really good for me to speak to other magazines.'

Kate's vegetarianism made her the natural choice as an un-official spokesperson for the anti-meat brigade, and she was happy to spread the word. She penned an article under the heading HOW CAN YOU EAT DEAD ANIMALS? for *Woman's World*, appeared on Delia Smith's television programme and later appeared on the cover of *Lean Living* ('The Meat Free Lifestyle').

On the Smith programme Bush revealed that she'd been a vegetarian since the mid-1970s. 'I think ever since I've been quite young I've always felt a bit guilty about eating meat,' she said. 'One day I just had this feeling and tried to eat a bit of meat and it was so raw that I just identified immediately with the fact that it was an animal. That this thing was alive and it had been killed for me to eat it and I thought, "No, I'm not into this." So I thought I'd become a vegetarian. I didn't have a clue, I had no idea what I could eat all I knew was that people didn't eat meat or fish. And I used to eat a lot of chocolate, so I lived for the next week off chocolate and tea.

'Eventually, through meeting other friends that were vegetarians and books and things, I managed to get a diet together. And it's fantastic, because when I ate meat I wouldn't touch vegetables, I hated them. But since I've become vegetarian I'll eat really only vegetables, you know. So it's really broadened my diet. Working in London I often have to go past meat markets and when I see all those people working in there with blood all over them and dead animals strung up from meat hooks, just waiting to be devoured, it's like something out of a horror film.'

Never For Ever became the first album by a British female solo artist to enter the charts at Number 1. This may have been helped by a magazine campaign in which cutting out a voucher entitled the reader to save money and buy the LP for a bargain price.

European sales were boosted by a sustained promotional campaign and a series of TV appearances across the continent. In Germany, France and Italy she gave performances of 'Babooshka' and the new single 'Army Dreamers'. The latter had a new video produced from a storyboard sketched by Kate herself. Kate and the band dressed as soldiers and were filmed in various scenes running through woods and dodging some primitive pyrotechnics. She said she'd been influenced by every war movie she'd ever seen, everything from *All Quiet on the Western Front* to *Apocalypse Now*, though few of those featured soldiers wearing as much lipstick and eye makeup as Kate did in this clip! The soldiers wore 'KT' patches on their shoulders and the producers employed a 'jerk jacket' to get the violent motion of soldiers being flung around from the explosions.

Bush ended the year all over the BBC. On TV's *Russell Harty Show* she took part in a special programme dedicated to the composer Delius; and on Radio 1, on the final two days of the year, she took part in two programmes with Paul Gambaccini in which she was interviewed, played live, discussed her favourite artists and picked a selection of music to be played, revealing admiration for Frank Zappa, Steely Dan and Captain Beefheart.

She was also in the news over possible TV and stage roles that had been offered to her. She was reportedly tempted by the offer of the part of a wicked witch in the children's TV series *Worzel Gummidge*. 'I was offered a part in a TV series,' she confirmed. 'I've been offered other acting roles but this was the first totally creative offer that has ever come my way. I had to turn it down – I was already committed to the album. Sadly I don't think that offer will be made again but you have to learn to let things go, not to hang on and get upset, or to try to do it and then end up making a mess of everything else.'

She also turned down an offer to play a leading role in the West End production of *The Pirates of Penzance*. Certain newspapers reported that she'd been offered parts in two horror movies. 'It's interesting to see how people cast you, but I don't think I'm anything like a vampire,' she smiled (obviously she hadn't watched her own 'Wuthering Heights' video then!). Other offers were equally unappealing. Early in her career another children's TV show offered her a role about the rise of a singer, but she didn't want to do something that had been done many times before. As usual, she would be doing what she wanted, when she wanted – and, after three hectic years, she felt it was time for a break.

Chapter Nine

Frightened of the Exposure

London and Sussex, 1981–83

'I wasn't sure what I wanted then and became frightened of the exposure. Being so vulnerable, I didn't know if I wanted to be famous or just make a record I was happy with. We moved to the country and that helped me relax. I am not the kind of person who enjoys living in London and I needed to get away and spend time on my life because until then I'd never stopped.'

KATE BUSH

WHEN BEING INSTALLED, the studio had partly closed up the lower, underground, portions of the building. This basement had originally housed a swimming pool, which was now been built over. But physically it was still there, sitting in its dark and dank atmosphere with its tiles collecting a layer of moss and a foot or two of water puddled at the deep end. Kate Bush had been recording here for a while and had decided she wanted an echoing environment for her latest vocal take. Displaying a perfectionism that was becoming legendary, she would go to extreme lengths if necessary to achieve the exact sounds that she wanted and would take as long as was needed to get it *just* right.

When she heard about the disused swimming pool in the basement it sounded perfect, so she wasted no time and clambered down into the disused space. She wanted to make sure that she got the sound of her voice reflecting off the water and making it sound as if she were on a river. The technicians and engineer set up the microphones and she sang her part, capturing it exactly as she'd envisioned it in her head. And all this for a humble B-side.

★   ★   ★

Often an artist that breaks through to mass acclaim with a debut album then has to contend with what is typically described as a 'difficult' second album. For Kate Bush the 'difficult' album was her fourth. From the earliest demos to the final released record, she took two years: the start of what would become a growing length of time between albums.

She'd begun working on her fourth album in the farm studio during August 1980, before *Never For Ever* had even been released, and she continued to work on it during breaks from her promotional duties during that autumn.

Bands such as Ultravox, Visage and Duran Duran were spreading the word of synth-pop through the UK charts. Visage producer Richard Burgess was also a member of the band Landscape, who released several early-1980s albums. It was Burgess who helped turn Kate Bush onto the use of synthesisers and samplers, namely the Fairlight CMI, after her introduction to this practice when she'd guested on Peter Gabriel's album earlier in the year.

Bush was still using the piano as her primary composing instrument but then 'translated' those melodies and programmed them into a synthesiser to allow her to add atmospheres and textures without the need for outside musicians to come in and record. Once she got to grips with the Fairlight she was happier because it produced 'very human, animal emotional sounds'. The atmospheric sounds of the Fairlight soon became a Kate Bush trademark. For this album she also used a Linn drum machine for the demos, but a real drummer was substituted for the actual recordings. By early 1981, she revealed that she'd produced 'a lot' of songs at her home studio and in May she was ready to go into a professional studio with her demos.

The first of what would amount to five studios to produce Kate Bush's fourth album was West London's Townhouse Studio Two. She had demos of around 20 songs, though only half that number would eventually be used on the album. The idea was that Kate would herself produce the album and use an experienced engineer to help her get the sounds she wanted.

Hugh Padgham had come to prominence for his work with XTC (*Black Sea*) and the Police (*Ghost in the Machine*). Just before he agreed to engineer Bush's album, Genesis had asked Padgham to produce their *ABACAB* album. So he found himself in the position of working for four days a week with Genesis and then three further days a week with Kate Bush. This was never going to be an arrangement that could last very long and the producer/engineer was soon exhausted. Though both parties were simultaneously happy with Padgham's work, he himself needed a day off every now and then, and because he had committed to Genesis first, he told Kate that he'd try to find someone to take over his engineering duties for her sessions.

The obvious choice for Padgham's recommendation was 20-year-old engineer Nick Launay. Launay had worked on a handful of albums before impressing ex-Sex Pistol John Lydon (Johnny Rotten) enough to be given the job of producing Public Image Limited's album *The Flowers of Romance*. 'Hugh heard some of the Public Image stuff, realised that I'd very quickly learned how to get those kind of big drum sounds, which were his thing, and I knew how to do it and got the whole vibe of that,' explains Launay today. 'So he suggested to Kate Bush that she should talk to me and maybe I should work with her because he couldn't. He played her the Public Image Limited album and I guess she must have liked it because a few days later I got asked to meet her. I was thrilled as you can imagine.'

Like many people, Launay had been taken aback when he'd first heard 'Wuthering Heights' on the radio. 'I then saw the video and felt hypnotised and taken into an another world,' he adds. 'I remember being very drawn to how her vocal builds and builds throughout that song. Her voice seems to float above the music in much the same way that she moves. I also love the characters she creates with her voice, and the way she gets into roles like an actor would in theatre.'

So, after working on just three songs, Padgham gave way to Launay, who continued working on the basic band tracks and vocals for several months more. Launay remembers the sessions being a lot of fun. He and Kate were of a similar age and he couldn't get over the fact that two people still relatively so young were left to their own devices to make whatever crazy sounds they wanted in the studio. 'I loved her imagination – it was like creating a fantasy world through sounds,' he says. 'I also remember her eating vast amounts of chocolate in clouds of smoke! She is very descriptive when explaining the mood and emotion she wants to get across with each instrument, and she describes things with great enthusiasm, so it was very easy for the musicians to grasp what she wanted.'

Often Bush's requests to Launay were quite unconventional and tested his recording skills to the limit. 'Some days I'd come in to great requests such as, "Nick, can we make the drums sound like distant cannons on the other side of the valley?"' he laughs. 'This ended up involving twelve-foot tubes of corrugated iron, with microphones placed inside at various distances. On one song, called "Lord of the Reedy River" [originally recorded by Donovan], she wanted it to sound like she was floating down a river. So she climbed into the cellar below the studio to do her vocal. The base-ment was originally a swimming pool that had been built over. It had about a foot of water in it so her voice reflected off it.'

As with most Kate Bush sessions, the working day began just after lunch and went on into the early hours of the following morning. Launay was always kept on his toes, running around like crazy, coming up with adventurous recording techniques and making sure everything was as set up and ready for the unknown as was possible. 'I felt it was my duty to catch all the wild ideas flying around Kate's head,' he says. 'Sometimes I felt like a butterfly catcher! Sometimes I needed three very big nets!'

The sense of the surreal and unknown intensified when Kate wondered out loud one day if she could find a didgeridoo player in England. Two days later she had obtained the number for Rolf Harris and gave him a call. He offered to play right away and arrived at the studio at nine o'clock that same night. As he walked in his first exchange with Nick Launay went like this:

Launay: 'How do you record a didgeridoo, Rolf?'

Harris: 'Dunno, mate, bung a couple of mikes up and let's see how she blows!'

Harris ended up teaching the breathing techniques for playing this long, pipelike Aboriginal instrument to Paddy Bush and giving him one as a gift. Apparently, Paddy is quite an accomplished player now. Harris also did a painting for Kate, which is on the back of one of the original analogue tape boxes from the session.

Other musicians working on the album were the now regular core of Ian Bairnson, Stuart Elliott and Del Palmer. Townhouse Studio Two had two recording rooms, neither of which was very big. Launay explains: 'One was carpeted and kind of dead-sounding with a small octagonal wood area, which was designed to be a drum booth in the 1970s. The other room has all stone surfaces and a very high ceiling. The stone room is extremely loud and live-sounding.'

This stone room is where Phil Collins's drum sound on 'In the Air Tonight' was conceived. It's also where Kate had sung on Peter Gabriel's album, which is probably why she chose it in the first place.

'In order to get more resonance,' recalls Launay, 'Kate's piano was placed on the only wooden area available, where she could also have good eye contact with the drummer in the stone room and me in the control room. The vocals were done in the carpeted area. It felt like we were pushing the boundaries. I think Kate is still one of the most influential innovators even today, and that LP is probably the best example of her imaginative mind. Kate is still to this day one of the most gifted people I've ever met. She was just born with incredible talents.' Considering that Launay has since worked with the likes of David Byrne, Midnight Oil, Gang of Four, Killing Joke, the Birthday Party, INXS and Nick Cave, that's high praise indeed.

In the three months at the Townhouse all of the basic tracks and instrumentation were recorded before Kate took the tapes back to the farm studio to work on further vocals and some overdubs.

In spring 1981 the *Sunday Telegraph* published an opinion poll that managed to place Kate Bush as both the country's 'most liked' and 'least liked' British female singer. This polarising of opinions would follow through to the new album but, in the meantime, the album was still a year away from being released, and EMI were more concerned with keeping Kate in the public eye. After she'd been closely followed for three years, even a few months of quiet from the Bush camp made it seem as though she'd slipped from the public's consciousness. New poster girls were popping up, and in the fast-changing world of UK pop you needed to keep pushing the singles out to stay on top. Both Altered Images' Clare Grogan and solo artist Kim Wilde scored big hits during the year.

So, a full year before the album would follow, EMI put out 'Sat In Your Lap' as a single in the summer of 1981. Backed with the aforementioned 'Lord of the Reedy River', the single stormed to Number 11 in the UK charts and was issued across Europe and in Australia. The song was a wild departure from Bush's previous work, as pounding drums set a furious pace.

The next port of call was the friendly confines of Abbey Road, where most of the backing tracks were completed with engineer Haydn Bendall, and it was here that the video for 'Sat In Your Lap' was filmed in June. Technically, the video was fairly straight-forward. Kate was filmed sitting on the floor making some wild arm motions while lip-synching and much of the rest of the video was taken up with roller-skating sequences featuring Kate and her two long-standing dance partners Gary Hurst and Stewart Avon-Arnold. Wearing white robes, an assortment of masks and a pointed 'dunce's' cap, they skated to the camera.

The first thing that hit listeners was the thumping drumbeat and chiming piano. Then came something unexpected: a semi-spoken Bush vocal through the verses that sounded unlike her previous singing. Then she let rip with a semi-operatic howl through the chorus. Another swing from the Bush norm was the electronic-sounding 'oohs' and 'ahs' and even a horn section. This wasn't the usual Kate Bush fare.

Bush also gave interviews and a TV appearance (on the children's show *Razzmatazz*) to talk about the new song and video. '[I've] been tucked away in the studio during the riots,' she quipped referring to the inner-city troubles taking place in England that summer. As a knowing prelude to the public's reaction to the album, the single confused quite a few people. 'I was really frightened about the single for a while,' she said. 'I mixed the song and played it to people, and there was complete silence afterwards, or else people would say they liked it to me and perhaps go away and say what they really thought. Of course it's really worrying, because there's an assumption that if you're one of us, an artist, you don't need feedback at all, when in fact you need it as much as ever, if not more. I really appreciate feedback, and I'm lucky that the people closest to me, my friends and family, are used to me and realise that I've got my own "bowl of feedback" to rely on. There will always be some who are irritated by me. I seem to irritate a lot of people, and in a way that's quite a good thing.'

A short trip to Dublin was arranged to record a track called 'Night of the Swallow'. After flirting with an Irish accent on 'Army Dreamers', Kate fully embraced her Irish roots with members of the Irish bands Planxty and the Chieftains. Back in England, another change of studio took Kate to Odyssey Studios, this time with Paul Hardiman as engineer, to work on overdubs of the basic tracks. As with all stages of this album, Kate wasn't going to rush, and these sessions took over three months into October. Having been working on the album on and off for a year now, Kate was approaching a state of exhaustion and called a much-needed halt to proceedings.

'Having worked so long on it I reached the point where I lost all impetus, something I have never experienced,' she wrote in the fan club newsletter. 'I found it hard to even listen to the tracks – some would call it saturation point.' For the last months of 1981 Kate kept away from the studio – to recharge mentally as much as anything. A trip to Loch Ness didn't afford her a view of its celebrated monster Nessie, but she did have a possible UFO sighting.

Fresh from her holiday, Bush dove into the final stages of the album with fresh vigour in January 1982. Paul Hardiman was continuing in his role as engineer for the final overdubs and then the mixing, all of which took place at Advision Studios. Advision, based on Gosfield Street in West London, had been, as the name suggests, a centre for recording advertisements until the 1970s, when it moved to more music-oriented endeavours. Jeff Wayne had famously recorded his epic *War of the Worlds* album there in 1978. Bush and Hardiman would spend over five months over-dubbing and mixing at the facility. She then flew off to Jamaica for a break, while preparations for a late July release were made.

In the week leading up to the album's release Kate was asked at very short notice to step in and replace David Bowie for a gala concert at the Dominion Theatre in London in aid of Prince Charles's Prince's Trust charity. Alongside those fellow chart toppers of the day, Madness, Bucks Fizz and Status Quo, Kate rehearsed with a hastily arranged band featuring the Who's Peter Townshend and Ultravox's Midge Ure on guitars, Genesis drummer Phil Collins, Gary Brooker from Procol Harum on keyboards and Japan's Mick Karn on bass. Bush performed 'The Wedding List' from the forthcoming album. Rather than write up the superstar ensemble's performance, though, the watching press pack found their headlines for the next day when Kate's top broke a strap mid-song and she had to complete the performance with arms crossed to preserve her dignity. Midge Ure was quoted as saying, 'Kate's toppling top was the highlight of the evening for me!' And Pete Townshend cheekily added, 'Her predicament just goes to show the power of prayer.'

The Dreaming was reviewed in *Melody Maker* as one of the weirdest records they'd ever heard. So what does it sound like almost 25 years later? The liner notes implore that this is an album 'made to be played loud', though why this should be more the case than *Never For Ever* is unclear. One thing that is very evident throughout the album is the range of different vocal styles that Bush uses – not to mention the accents and enunciations that she experiments with, which veer wildly from the sublime to the ridiculous.

'I stretched the pitch range over the years,' she explained then. 'What I used to do in my earlier performances was to go for notes higher than I could easily reach in the song. So by the time I'd written the song and played it for a good few days I could actually reach those notes. Definitely my voice has got stronger over the last two years. On *The Dreaming* it was much stronger but also more controlled. My use of decorative notes comes from Irish music and in my childhood my brothers were very into traditional music and we could hear it in the house all the time.'

Her electronic experiments and adventures are all over the album. Perhaps too much so, because, while she brings an earthy feel to some tracks with tribal rhythms ranging from Ireland to

Australia, the sound is often quite plastic compared with her early work. On other tracks, though, the songwriting and production is exemplary. She'd used so many different studios because she wanted certain facilities for certain tracks and had to fit in around other artists who'd already booked in. Everything on the album had been assembled quite mechanically in layers, unlike early recordings, which had been real performances in the studio. First, all the basic backing tracks were recorded. Then she added layers with other musicians. Then it was her own vocals, which for a single song could take weeks at a time. Then she added the Fairlight on top of everything.

Was she successful with this approach? Sometimes. Would some outside control have improved the production of the album? Probably. At some times the collection is simply breathtaking and at other times it's bewildering because a great idea is just pushed past the point of self-indulgence into an intricate web of confusion. But she couldn't be faulted for being brave with her conviction and following a path that she alone wanted to travel.

'The LP for me has been quite fulfilling,' she said at the time. 'I feel I have made a step forward, which is always great for one artistically, obviously. And I suppose one of the things that I do feel pleased about is perhaps that I feel we've got a sense of the emotional value from each song to have come across in some way. It was very emotionally demanding, especially some of the tracks, because of the subject matter. The songs started growing and changing in the studios, something that's never happened on any of my other albums.'

The surprise opening of 'Sat In Your Lap' was compounded by the follow-up of 'There Goes a Tenner', swinging between a comedy 'mockney' accent, a high-pitched, girly refrain and a well-spoken brogue. The swaying, horn-driven melody carries the narrative of a bank raid or robbery gone wrong. The schizophrenic vocals are at ease with the similarly twisting moods of the songs. The chugging melody frequently breaks down into gentle interludes.

'It's sort of all the films I've seen with robberies in,' she said. 'The crooks have always been incredibly in control and calm, and I always thought that, if I ever did a robbery, I'd be really scared, you know, I'd be really worried. So I thought I'm sure that's a much more human point of view.'

'Pull Out the Pin' was similarly inspired by TV. This time it was a documentary she'd seen about the USA's involvement in Vietnam. For a change it was written from a Vietnamese point of view and featured *Apocalypse Now*-style helicopter effects and a guest appearance by Dave Gilmour on backing vocals. 'There was a fantastic TV documentary about a cameraman who was on the front lines,' explained Bush. 'He was a brilliant cameraman and he was so well trained a technician that he kept filming things no matter how he was feeling about it at the time. Some of the stuff he was shooting was really disturbing. Some of the Vietnamese guys would just come in and they were sort of dying in midair. And he'd just keep on filming.'

'Suspended in Gaffa' was a successful overseas single release but was passed over by EMI in the UK for some reason. Its fairground-organ feel bounces along but the lyric is difficult to decipher. 'Lyrically, it's not really that dissimilar from "Sat In Your Lap" in saying that you really want to work for something,' Bush explained. 'It's playing with the idea of hell. At school I was always taught that if you went to hell you would see a glimpse of God and that was it – you never saw him again and you'd spend the rest of eternity pining to see him.'

Side One closed with the metronomic 'Leave It Open', which gave the world some of the weirdest Bush vocals to date. Bush was quoted as saying of the song, '[It's] the idea of human beings being like cups, like receptive vessels. We open and shut ourselves at different times.' Kate apologists have argued that this particular track needs an open mind for it to be fully appreciated – but even being a Kate fan and having an open mind doesn't disguise the fact that it isn't really very good.

By stark contrast, Side Two opens with the title track, 'The Dreaming', which, though dense, repays the time spent listening. This time the semi-comedy vocal is sung in an Australian accent. The opening car-crash sounds are all Fairlight-produced and the layers of Paddy Bush's droning bullroarer and Rolf Harris's didgeridoo swirl and hum. The animal impersonator Percy Edwards makes sheep noises in the break. The song focuses on the plight of the Aborigines in Australia and more generally on indigenous races around the world that have almost been wiped out by white colonial rule. Bush said she'd never visited the outback but was sure it would be everything she 'dreamed' it would be. 'I started to become aware of the whole thing,' she said. 'It's almost an instinctive thing in white man to wipe out a race that actually owns the land. It's happening all around the world.

'I'd been trying to get some kind of tribal drum sound together for a couple of albums, especially the last one. But really the problem was that I was trying to work with a pop medium and get something out of it that wasn't part of that setup.'

'Night of the Swallow' takes the album's journey from Australia to Ireland. With members of Planxty and the Chieftains, a decidedly Irish feel is produced by bouzouki, uilleann pipes and penny whistle. 'They're fantastic musicians with open, receptive minds, which is unusual for people who work with traditional folk music,' said Bush.

'All the Love' is a piano-led track that pauses for a heavenly interlude provided by choirboy Richard Thornton. 'Houdini' brings in Eberhard Weber on bass for the story of Houdini and Rosabel, as depicted on the album's cover. Another guest on this track was Kate's old singing teacher Gordon Farrell. 'Years ago I used to go every week for these lessons, and really it was great,' says Bush. 'He gave me loads of confidence in singing, which is what I needed more than anything. I just used to go to him half an hour a week, and by the end of the year I felt a lot more confident in myself as a singer. He worked wonders! And on Houdini at the end there are these sounds, and that's him.'

The closing 'Get Out of My House' unwittingly captures the whole album in one short passage of its lyric. It screams, 'This house is full of my mess/this house is full of my mistakes/ this house is full of my madness . . .' The album is disjointed, containing mistakes and (with a closing salvo of 'eeyores') it has its fair share of madness, too!

'The idea with that song is that the house is actually a human being who's been hurt and he's just locking all the doors and not letting anyone in,' explains Bush. 'The person is so determined not to let anyone in that one of his personalities is a concierge who sits in the door and says, "You're not coming in here."' And so it ends.

Overall, *The Dreaming* probably tries too hard to be too many things at once. From the Cockney bank raid to the wander through the Australian outback, to Ireland, to the war in Vietnam and with the story of Houdini thrown in for good measure, it's a lot to take in. Add to this the fact that musically the album is quite a challenge to listen to and you get a collection that put off many casual listeners.

'It has been very hard to produce because all the studios are so incredibly booked up, and because I wanted to use one engineer only,' said Bush at the time. 'This is the first album that I have produced myself, which meant a great deal more responsibility for me. As soon as you get your hands on the production it becomes your baby. I seemed to be losing sight of my direction. I really wasn't sure what to do next – and that hasn't happened to me before.'

Nick Launay had gone away from his part of the production process without knowing what to expect from the finished product. When he finally heard the whole thing a year and a half later he was surprised. 'I thought it was amazing, and still do,' he says. 'Some songs didn't change much, while others changed quite a lot. Sonically, I do remember thinking the mixes sounded a bit odd at first, and not as warm as I remembered it being. Later I came to realise that this was because it had been mixed to a then new format called "digital". *The Dreaming* was one of the first albums ever to be mixed to digital. Being early days of this technology, it was a bit sonically brittle. Musically and production-wise, I think it's a masterpiece.'

'*The Dreaming* is very different from my first two records,' Kate concludes. 'Each time I do an album it feels like the last one was years and years before. The essence of what I'm playing has been there from the start. It's just that the expression has been changing. What I'm doing now is what I was trying to do four years ago. If I do a show, it will only be music from the last two albums. I wish I had a five-year plan, but I never plan too far ahead. I get into trouble because I always take longer to do things than I expect. That's why I knew I had to wait for another two albums' worth of material before doing another show.'

However, the 'next' show never materialised, and nor did a lot of backing from EMI. No doubt the label was just as perplexed by her latest offering as most of the press and much of the public were. They seemed to want to cut their losses on the project and held back on giving the album much of a promotional push aside from some magazine adverts and vouchers allowing buyers to purchase the record for a discounted price, which, unlike the case with *Never For Ever*, had little effect on sales, with no high-riding single to help out. 'Sat In Your Lap', though a successful single, seemed to have been forgotten, because it had been released a year before the album that contained it.

The press were scathing in their dismissal of the album and, though some Kate fans have hailed the album as her masterpiece, the truth is that it lies somewhere between these two extremes. It didn't fit in with the pop moods of the times and the early 1980s were a particularly vacuous time in UK rock and pop. The album wasn't as bad as reported and, with the admitted advantage of

20-plus years of hindsight, it is revealed as an ambitious but ultimately flawed attempt to reinvent Bush as a more serious and stylised writer and producer. The problem is that her mistakes were made in public and recorded on the album for all to pore over in the future.

The album cover showed a close-up photograph of Kate leaning forward to kiss a man who appears to be in chains with a padlock in the foreground. In her open mouth she seems to be resting a ring on her tongue. Look closer and you'll see it's actually a key. The whole concept is linked to the song 'Houdini', and here she is re-enacting Houdini's wife giving her daredevil husband some help in one of his daring escapes. Kate explained, 'That song is taken from Mrs Houdini's point of view, because she spent a lot of time working with him and helping with his tricks. One of the ways she would help was to give him a parting kiss, just as he was off into his water tank or whatever, and as she kissed him she'd pass a tiny little key which he would then use later to unlock the padlocks. I thought it was both a very romantic and a very sad image because, by passing that key, she is keeping him alive. She's actually giving him the key back into life. As soon as I heard that imagery, I just thought it was so beautiful, and so extraordinary.'

To promote the album, the eponymous single was issued in July 1982 but the weird subject matter, strange production and lack of radio airplay conspired to stop its progress at a lowly Number 48 in the singles chart. The album faired better, but not by much. Some reviews were good but often writers were mystified that she had produced such a strange record in comparison with her first three albums. The fact that she'd produced it herself was often brought up as a factor in the adjudged lack of 'quality control' and editing on the album. The record-buying public also found it inaccessible on a few hearings and it sold poorly relative to her others.

As part of the promotional duties for *The Dreaming*, Kate undertook the usual rounds of record-store appearances and TV interviews. She also worked out dance routines for several TV shows at home and abroad. For *The Old Grey Whistle Test* she travelled up by train to the studios in Manchester in an empty goods wagon, where she rehearsed her dance routines. 'A lot of my movements come from my training,' she explained then. 'During that time Robin Kovak at the Dance Centre had a big influence on me. She certainly gave me the strength to develop my own style. I now do my dance rehearsals in a small studio near my home and I have a set group of dancers that I can call upon to work with.'

Kate put most of her promotional energies into making videos for the singles from the album, but her efforts pretty much fell flat. 'There Goes a Tenner' was her lowest-selling single so far and received little radio and TV coverage. The video revolved around scenes of the botched robbery with Del Palmer making a brief cameo as the gang's getaway driver.

The video for 'Suspended in Gaffa' was a return to a single dance-routine video, with virtually no extras and few special effects. Sitting on the floor and flailing around as she did at the start of the 'Sat In Your Lap' clip, Bush then pranced around a barn in what could only be described as a morris dancer's or court jester's style. Later, a brief cameo is made by her mother Hannah. Kate's hairstyle (which was a cross between A Flock Of Seagulls and Limahl!) today makes her seem strangely modern due to the current 1980s retro-mania.

Both of these videos had little UK TV coverage, although 'Suspended in Gaffa' did get some airtime on the new MTV channel, which by now already had a staggering 14 million viewers, though even that pales in comparison with today's estimated worldwide audiences of more than 50 times that number! In overseas markets this single sold well.

In the USA *The Dreaming* was released by EMI America and was boosted by support on college radio, where she received some glowing reviews. Despite good reviews around the globe, the UK sales were very disappointing compared with those of the first three albums, and the mediocre chart positions attained by her singles (though 'Sat In Your Lap' had reached Number 11, 'The Dreaming' faltered at Number 48 and 'There Goes a Tenner' failed to chart at all) were a massive setback, especially after she'd spent so long meticulously preparing, recording and mixing the album.

In 1983 Kate disappeared from public view. She need to rethink her career and her life. For the best part of six years she'd been swept along on a wave of fame and acclaim but now she'd encountered the first negative feedback of her career, despite putting her heart and soul into what in hindsight is a very dense album. She was now 24 years old and the majority of her adult life to date had been something of a blur.

During 1983 she moved out of London to a cottage on the Sussex coast, where she enjoyed the best summer since 1976. She had also had the farm studio upgraded. As she took stock of her life she realised that she didn't have to be shy about having vast amounts of money at her disposal now.

'I've changed. I don't pretend it's not there any more, which I used to do,' she said of her growing bank balance. 'I'm not worried about being rich. I just didn't think of taking advantage of it. Now I buy things that I can use, things that will help me, like synthesisers and drum machines. My life has never been into money, more into emotional desires. Like being an incredible singer or an incredible dancer, and, if I can buy something that can help me, I will now. But I wouldn't buy something that I couldn't live with, like a country house which I don't need. I'd rather buy a huge synthesiser that I could live with all day.'

Taking time off allowed her to regain a sense of being human again. She was undoubtedly feeling more than a little bemused about the sales of *The Dreaming*. She always held a strong belief in her own judgements but this time they seemed to have missed the mark. Or was it a stubborn case of 'I'm right and the world is wrong'? Either way, she enjoyed the normality of just going to the shops, visiting the cinema, taking long walks and visiting friends in her VW Beetle. The endless stream of interviews and being holed up in the studio wasn't missed at all. 'That time I took off in 1983 was reorganising everything,' she said in 1985. 'I've made some of the best decisions in the last two years.'

In Sussex she worked on a new fitness regime, cut out the junk food and takeaways that were becoming her staple diet while working at the studio and she enlisted Dianne Gray as her new dance teacher. By September she was feeling better and had started writing for her next album.

Chapter Ten

Make That Evolution

England, 1984-85

'I watched her technique develop over the many years I worked with her, the operative word being "with". She relies on creative input from those around her. Having said that, she knows what she wants, and also knows what she likes as *soon* as she has heard it! But sometimes we would thrash around on various ideas before coming up with the final cut. Often I would end up doing something close to what I started out with! But that doesn't mean the creative processes in between were not useful. It needed to make that evolution.'

CHARLIE MORGAN

KATE BUSH'S NEXT ALBUM WOULD throw her squarely back into the limelight of mass acclaim. She really was becoming commented on as some kind of national treasure, deeply woven into the fabric of British society. In years to come she would be a regular for contestants on the celebrity imitation 'talent' show, *Stars in Their Eyes*; Pamela Stephenson had spoofed Kate on BBC2's comedy show, *Not The Nine O'Clock News*; comedian/impersonator Faith Brown did a surprisingly good send-up of Bush singing 'Wow'; and the new album would provide a whole medley's worth of comic material for comedian Steve Coogan. The public seemed to forgive her experimentation on *The Dreaming* and welcomed her back into the mainstream with open arms, as she released what would be her most successful album to date.

★   ★   ★

The fact that *The Dreaming* had dramatically underwhelmed commercial expectations and that Kate had kept a low profile for a year or so has been held up by some parts of the media as proof that her career was about to come crashing down. Many rumours circulated and, among other things, they claimed that she'd put on lots of weight and was about to part company with EMI. As usual all of these things were exaggerated, some by bigger margins than others. She did put on weight while working for months in the studio with little exercise – too many takeaways and chocolate saw to that – but she hadn't ballooned in size as some writers would have us believe. Her career had hit a blip with *The Dreaming* but she wasn't about to fall apart. And, yes, she wasn't seeing eye to eye with EMI over their handling of her output, nor they with her over what she was producing for them to promote.

Spiralling studio costs for the ever-lengthening time it was taking her to record an album meant the company, understandably, would want a bigger return on its investment. When *The Dreaming* failed to deliver back on that investment there must have been questions raised in the EMI corridors of power. To her credit Bush saw this coming and the upgrading of her home studio would shield her from time constraints and expensive studio bills in the future. 'The way I work is very experimental,' she said. 'When you know the studio is costing a phenomenal amount of money every hour it just zaps creativity.'

Between *The Dreaming* and the follow-up album, which wouldn't be released until three years later in 1985, she not only made changes to her working environment, but he also saw personnel changes at EMI that meant she would have a new contact there in the form of one David Munns. He has since been credited with making her 'comeback' in 1985 much easier, and his ensuring that she was given full company support paved the way to her commercial rebirth on both sides of the Atlantic.

'I've made some of my best decisions in the last two years,' Bush said at the time, rather cryptically, of her break between albums. 'I have to go back to the work because that's what matters. Work obsesses my life and everyone around me is dragged into it. It's terrible, really.'

In January 1984 Bush was present for the launch of the UK's first satellite channel – Sky TV. Linked with the MTV-led rise of specialist music channels such as Music Box and VH-1, the launch of Sky gave a foothold for the format that eventually led to the loss of importance of *Top of the Pops* and a massive rise for the creative and economical worth of the pop video. These promotional clips came to be seen as a standalone art form at best and as a poor-quality commercial for run-of-the-mill pop at worst. The growth of videos as promotional tools allowed Bush to exploit the new expanding medium to put her dance and visual side across to large audiences instead of touring. EMI also agreed to put funds into her video budgets instead of holding them back for possible tour support.

While she was tentatively beginning work on the next album EMI released a collector's box of seven-inch singles covering her whole career to date and an accompanying video, *The Single File*, which topped the music video charts. The 12 promo videos included on the tape showcased the evolution of her work from the initial simplicity of 'Wuthering Heights'. 'Songs have very specific moods and personalities,' she says. 'I feel very limited in as much as I'm always, to a certain extent, me. I'm never sure if I'm able to create the character in the song. I really rely on my instincts because I don't feel I can act. It's the subject matter, not the personalities, that moves me. Though it could apply to any kind of art and the character is an actor, it's really talking about the music business where a lot of things are really unpleasant, but the incredible thing about it is the music and how it's worth all the effort, all the rubbish, to get that bit of gold.' From the soft-focused 'The Man With The Child In His Eyes', to the dramatic 'Breathing' and beyond to her mini-movies, the growth of Kate Bush the filmmaker is plain to see.

Having had to use five different studios to finally see *The Dreaming* through to completion, and shoulder the hassle from EMI over the costs that that project incurred, she felt the next logical step was to remove these costs from the next album. So the farm studio was upgraded during late 1983 to a professional 48-track facility. Designed and built to Kate's exact specifications, though state-of-the-art technology was financially out of the question, it was still a viable recording facility. Unusually, Bush wanted a windowless recording room, not even a panel through to the control room. All control to studio communication was done via microphones and headsets. This arrangement must have helped her focus on the task at hand but it didn't mean things were accomplished any faster. If anything, things were so relaxed that they got slower and slower.

When the time came to start work on the new album that would become *Hounds of Love* in January 1984 she also had to take the stand that she would again produce it herself despite murmurs that she'd lost the plot on *The Dreaming*. 'I think it was probably the most difficult stage I've been at so far,' she explains, 'because [with] *The Dreaming*, I'd never produced an album before that one; and because it had a lot of unfavourable attention from some people, I think it was felt that my producing *Hounds of Love* wasn't such a good idea.

'And for the first time I felt I was actually meeting resistance artistically. I felt the album had done very well to reach Number Three, but I felt under a lot of pressure and I wanted to stay as close to my work as possible. And everyone was saying, "Oh, she's really gone mad now." But it was very important that it happened to me because it made me think, "Right, do I really want to produce my own stuff?" You know, "Do I really care about being famous?" And I was very pleased with myself that, no, it didn't matter as much as making a good album. The pressure of knowing the astronomical amount studio time cost used to make me really nervous about being too creative. You can't experiment for ever, and I work very, very slowly. I feel a lot more relaxed emotionally now that I have my own place to work and a home to go to.'

So, with full control, no time pressures and a relaxed environment, Kate began slowly demoing new material. In another break from previous practices she kept good original demo takes and, instead of later trying to recreate them, she built layers of overdubs onto the original takes. It would be 18 months until the album was actually released to the public.

Early stages of recording included just Kate and the ever-present Del Palmer engineering. Palmer's role in Bush's recorded output shouldn't be overlooked. He would always be the first at the studio every day, switching everything on and getting the place 'warmed up'. After he'd cleaned the recording heads and set up any equipment for visiting musicians, they'd be ready to start work at lunchtime. In the early throes of recording, his input was even more important, since he was also responsible for programming the Linn drum machine that was used on more than 20 early demos. As things progressed Paul Hardiman was again called upon to engineer and free up Palmer to play bass and sing backing vocals on five tracks. Once all the Fairlight parts had been laid down, Kate would choose which she wanted to be replaced by 'real' instruments. Drummer Stuart Elliott was one of the first musicians to play on the sessions. '[His] drumming is the most emotional I know,' says Bush. 'He's always interested in the songs and the lyrics and has a way of creating the right mood for a track.' There were some difficulties in turning the drum machine tracks to Stuart's own, and so sometimes they kept the machine and he worked in and around it.

Charlie Morgan also came in later to drum on five tracks for the album. 'He's very open-minded and is well up to date on all the latest drum-sampling equipment, and also happens to be a great drummer,' says Bush. Morgan spent several days working on the album and would drive down to the farm for a day here and a day there with a car full of equipment each time.

In the farm environment, Kate was more confident about making sure she got the sounds she wanted from the musicians around her. One morning Morgan arrived to find a whole assortment of drums piled up waiting for his arrival. On the day that they recorded a demo of 'The J' he had to play a whole host of snare drums, tenor drums, a large Northern Irish instrument called a lambeg drum, and a couple of bodhráns. On his arrival, Kate greeted Morgan with the words, 'I want this track to sound like an Irish army on the march.'

'I took a crash course in bodhrán,' laughs Morgan. 'That's something that has stayed with me the rest of my life, and we filled an entire 24-track slave tape with drums! I remember doing the first couple of tracks on snare drum, and messing around with stick hits on the rims. As soon as I did that, Kate came on the intercom saying, "Great, let's double that!" Of course, I had to then memorise where I had done the original rim shots! They would often "run through in record mode", which meant they would capture all the messing around we did. Then came the job of recreating it! The original demo sessions were amongst the most exciting, and experimental sessions I have played on. We were really breaking new ground. Anything was possible.'

After a day's worth of recording, the call would inevitably go out for an Indian takeaway (or Dr Bush would rustle up a steak dinner) and the assembled workers would gather round to listen through the day's tapes before making any changes and additions late at night.

'I have such wonderful memories of that time,' recalls Morgan. 'Recording with Kate and Del was almost like a refuge from all the other craziness going on in the outside world. It's as if time stood still. There was a magic about the farm that made everything slow down in pace. Languid, that's the best way to describe it. Throughout the day there would be little interruptions. The Doc would drop in, pipe in mouth, and pass the time of day. Hannah would arrive with a tray of tea things, asking how everything was going. Paddy would pop his head round the door, and often stay for a while. If John was around, he would invariably pay us a visit.

'I can't think of a better place in which to be creative. But you had to hang your watch up at the door! We were definitely in a time warp. So different from the regimented world of sessions, where you had to get it right almost immediately. We were being truly experimental. Sometimes we would try four or five different things on a track before deciding what worked.'

This immense attention to detail spread to even the seemingly most minor things. Between two of the tracks there was to be a segue of the sound of waves, but Bush decided the sound effects didn't sound like 'the right kind of sea', and so the section had to be redone.

'It was a fantastic place to work,' agrees engineer Haydn Bendell. 'You'd go next door and see her parents. Cup of tea and a sandwich. Lots of discussion around the kitchen table.' Everyone agreed that working at the farm was a pleasurable experience, even if Bush was struggling to be in a good mood. 'If she's having a bad day you will be the last to know about it,' reveals Stuart Elliott. 'She comes into the studio and smiles and it's all bright, airy and sunshine. She really does care about people.'

She could also show two completely different personae: from herself to whatever character she was portraying in a song. 'She's quietly spoken and petite,' explains Haydn Bendell. 'She'd be beside you in the control room chatting away and then step through into the booth and this amazingly powerful, passionate voice would come out, every fibre of her being committed to it. She was using her voice in a completely unashamed way.'

It wasn't just the music that progressed at a snail's pace, either. Bush was having difficulties coming up with the right words and the lyric writing came to stop on more than one occasion. To break the routine she and Palmer travelled to Ireland for some inspiration and booked into Windmill Lane Studios.

Windmill Lane had opened in 1978 and its comfortable surroundings quickly made it Ireland's number-one recording facility. The listed, Art Deco building had previously been part of the Dublin tram system, a Bovril factory and a snooker and amusement club. Today it's most famous for being the studio of choice for U2.

Bill Whelan took charge of the Irish sessions, notably on the tracks 'Jig of Life' and 'Hello Earth'. Kate said 'Not only was Bill a dream to work with but he made us feel very at home and we got to see Ireland in a really fun way.'

Liam O'Flynn and Donal Lunny from Planxty and John Sheahan, fiddle player from the Dubliners, made these tracks their own before backing vocals were added back in England. The 44-year-old German jazz bassist/cellist/composer Eberhard Weber was drafted in to play bass on two songs over two days after being sent a cassette with lyric sheet and notes. He provided his own bass parts to 'Hello Earth' and 'Mother Stands for Comfort'.

'She called me when I was in Hamburg,' says Weber. 'I couldn't even believe it was her. The hotel had a message from Kate Bush and I called her back. She told me she loved my music in particular.' Weber soon flew over to join the sessions, but they were far from what he had expected. Usually, his jazz sessions took two or three days, in which he would record and mix a whole album. He estimated it would take a couple of hours to record his part for the first song and then maybe another hour for the second.

'They checked every note – everything, everything, everything,' he laughs. 'The first tune took six to eight hours. The second one

Kate performing in London – she could be quite scary when she wanted to be.

Kate filming the TV clip for 'The Wedding List' section of the *Pebble Mill* Christmas special.

Kate with long-time beau Del Palmer, snapped here in 1985.

Kate and Peter Gabriel, who dueted with her on 'Don't Give Up'.

Dancer, Lindsay Kemp. An inspiration to Kate and David Bowie amongst many others.

Bass-playing collaborator Eberhard Weber feels his music.

The Trio Bulgarka brought their special vocal talents to *The Sensual World* and *The Red Shoes* albums.

Kate prepares herself for another run-through of 'The Big Sky' during a video shoot in March 1986

Kate thanks the fans for volunteering to work as extras during the video shoot of 'The Big Sky'.

Kate poses shortly after the release of her album *The Sensual World*.

Kate celebrates her 30th birthday in 1988. She spent the day doing charity work for an AIDS foundation.

Kate in March 2005. Here she is photographed at a reception to honour Britain's Music Industry at Buckingham Palace. The event was also attended by the likes of Shirley Bassey, Brian May and Phil Collins.

the same. It explained to me why these pop people take so long to produce their albums. They never decide right away what to do. So, when I came up with some ideas, they said, "Yes, yes, let's record it to 48 tracks." Then I'd have another idea and again, it would be "Yes, yes, yes, let's do it this way." I recorded tens of ideas and in the end, only one was accepted. These people have the attitude that it's only later when they mix that they decide. This is very unusual compared to the older productions in the 1970s when I started.'

Bush also wanted to add a layer of strings to several tracks. Her love of Pink Floyd's *The Wall* led to her asking that album's James Guthrie to engineer the string players. On an extremely hot, humid day the strings were recorded and between takes everyone would rush outside to breathe in the slightly less hot humid air and return to the inside to continue the recording.

In June the basic recording was complete and a mammoth 12 months of overdubbing and mixing were begun. Bush would work on new additions with Del Palmer for two or three days and then bring in Haydn Bendell to polish it up; and then she'd go back for new input with Del and repeat the process over and over. In the summer of 1985 it was finally done.

It may have taken three years between albums, but the wait was worth it. While *The Dreaming* did have its merits, that album's try-everything attitude was a stepping stone to greater things. Now *Hounds of Love* showed what Kate Bush the producer could really come up with: a highly structured, focused and melodic album that had hit singles all over it and meshed the electronic composition elements she'd now fully embraced with traditional instruments and arrangements. Lyrically it was an aural feast and the comedy voices (whether they were meant to be funny or not) were jettisoned.

Structurally, the album is a masterwork, though the advent of CDs has made it lose some of its potency as the songs are not separated by the end of Side One. The first side contained five standalone songs, which linked together through the theme of love and relationships under the overall title *Hounds of Love*, while the second side put forth a seven-song suite that was a complete work called *The Ninth Wave*.

As with much of her work, Bush was inspired by film and literature when writing the album. The title track drew from the 1957 film *Night of the Demon*; 'Cloudbusting' came from a book by the son of Wilhelm Reich; and *The Ninth Wave* collated ideas and images from a clutch of war and disaster movies.

The album opens with the ethereal Fairlight drone of 'Running Up That Hill' and a memorable drum track originally programmed by Del Palmer, but played for real by Stuart Elliott on the album. The basic premise of the song is that the man and woman in it can't understand each other because of their respective genders, and so it's proposed that they make a deal with God for them to swap places so that each can see things from the other's perspective. 'I thought a deal with the devil,' says Bush. 'Then I thought, "Well, no, why not a deal with God!" Because in a way it's so much more powerful, the whole idea of asking God to make a deal with you. You see, for me it is still called "Deal with God", that was its title.' Bush's vocal performance is outstanding on the track. Both authoritative and emotionally vulnerable, she spins a web of intrigue.

'Hounds of Love' was one of the first songs written for the album, when Bush became fascinated by the imagery of love as a physical thing that could hunt you down. The opening spoken line ('It's in the trees, it's coming') is taken from the film *Night of the Demon*. The song's character is running away from responsibility, scared of being in a relationship. 'The whole idea of being chased by this love that actually when it gets you it's just going to rip you to pieces, and have your guts all over the floor! So this being hunted by love – I liked the imagery, I thought it was really good.' This was another powerful vocal performance by Kate.

'The Big Sky' featured the Killing Joke bassist Youth and was a song that morphed in the studio to something quite different from the original demo. The underlying idea for the song was the hours that the young Kate Bush would spend just watching clouds up in the sky. She'd look for shapes that resembled animals and maps and suchlike and wait for them to change into the shape of something else. While writing the early songs for the album, Bush and Palmer were still living in the countryside and Kate's composing room overlooked a valley. Here she saw the clouds changing the lighting and atmosphere of the valley and was taken back to her youth. 'I knew what I wanted to finish up with, but I didn't seem to be able to get there! We had three different versions and eventually it just kind of turned into what it did.' The big drum sound they created was very much of its time in the mid-1980s.

'Mother Stands for Comfort' slows the pace right down and after the opening three-song salvo, which is wild and airy, the mood becomes quite dark. The mother in question is protecting a child who has done something terrible but the mother's naturally protective instincts come to the fore. 'The personality that sings this track is very unfeeling in a way,' explains Bush. 'The cold qualities of synths and machines were appropriate here. There are many different kinds of love and the track's really talking about the love of a mother, and in this case she's the mother of a murderer, in that she's basically prepared to protect her son against anything. In a way it's also suggesting that the son is using the mother, as much as the mother is protecting him.' It is sung from the point of view of the child, and the spooky atmospheric soundscape benefits from Eberhard Weber's understated bass work and the ever-present Fairlight.

Like 'Running Up That Hill', 'Cloudbusting' was propelled along by a great melody. This time the thrust is initially provided by a sublime string section performed by the Medici Sextet and arranged by Dave Lawson. The song was inspired by a book that Bush had bought years before in 1976, just because she liked the title and the cover, but she'd not read it until many years later. The book in question, Peter Reich's *Book of Dreams*, told of the author's early life with his father the controversial psychoanalyst and physician Wilhelm Reich.

Wilhelm Reich was an Austrian by birth and in the mid-1930s claimed to have discovered 'orgone energy', a purported force that he said could be found in the human body and throughout nature. After transferring his work to the United States just as World War Two broke out, he set up Orgonon on a 160-acre site in Maine, which housed his research headquarters.

One of his most ambitious projects was his 'cloudbuster' machine, which, he claimed, was able change atmospheric weather patterns, and, for example, cause rain when none was forecast. His most famous use of the machine was in 1953, when some local farmers offered him money to make it rain and save their blueberry crop. Within two days two inches of rain had fallen.

In an era when the McCarthy hearings were becoming the biggest US witch hunt of the twentieth century, no one was safe from government accusations. Wilhelm Reich certainly wasn't, and soon the federal authorities were on his trail, saying that orgone energy didn't exist. Instead of being engaged in a thought-out scientific debate, Reich was pursued through the courts and eventually arrested. In 1956 more than 20,000 of his publications were burned in New York in one of the country's biggest censorship operations. The following year he died in a federal penitentiary at the age of 59, having been convicted of making fraudulent claims.

Books of Dreams was written from a child's viewpoint. Peter Reich saw his father as a mystical, magical figure and it immediately struck a chord with Bush. 'One of the things that feature in the book is how he used to go with his father cloudbusting,' recalls Bush. 'His father had this machine that when you pointed it up to the sky you could make the clouds disperse or you could gather them together, and if you gathered them together it would rain. And the machine is all based on orgone energy, which is one of the bases of Reich's teachings. And the book is just extraordinary. It's so sad, but it's also got this beautiful kind of happy innocence that goes with childhood. And, as the guy grows up in the book, it does get sadder and sadder as you can feel him hanging onto his childhood. And the book really touched me, and the song is really trying to tell that story.'

One problem was the ending of the song. It didn't fade out or stop abruptly: it just sort of 'fell apart'. 'The drummer would stop and then the strings would just sort of start wiggling around and talking,' says Bush. 'I felt it needed an ending, and I didn't really know what to do. And then I thought maybe decoy tactics were the way, and we covered the whole thing over with the sound of a steam engine slowing down so that you had the sense of the journey coming to an end. And it worked, it covered up all the falling apart and actually made it sound very complete in a way.

'And we had terrible trouble getting a sound effect of steam train, so we actually made up the sound effect out of various sounds, and Del was the steam. [Laughs.] And we got a whistle on the Fairlight for the "poo poop".'

Before the album was finished Bush tracked down Peter Reich and sent him a copy of the song for his approval. 'I thought it would be really rude not to before the song came out,' she says. 'He liked it, which is great because I was really worried. I don't know what I'd have done if he didn't like it.'

Originally, listeners would have to stand up, or sit down, and turn over the record, or tape, before being plunged into *The Ninth Wave*. Wanting to prepare what amounts to a 25-minute piece of music as opposed to a four- or five-minute song presented a whole new set of challenges for Bush. As she had done in the past, she viewed the music as a piece of film (a later plan to film a short movie set to the music was scrapped). The narrative of the whole second side of the album is that of a girl who was been deposited in the sea, whether from a shipwreck or storm we don't know. She's waiting to die.

'I find that horrific imagery,' says Bush. 'The thought of being completely alone in all this water. And they've got a life jacket with a little light so that if anyone should be travelling at night they'll see the light and know they're there. And they're absolutely terrified, and they're completely alone at the mercy of their imagination, which again I personally find such a terrifying thing, the power of one's own imagination being let loose on something like that. And the idea that they've got it in their head that they mustn't fall asleep, because if you fall asleep when you're in the water, I've heard that you roll over and so you drown, so they're trying to keep themselves awake.'

Thus *The Ninth Wave* tells the story of the girl in the water, from her trying to stay awake through dreams of her past, present and possible future. Many of the lyrics were written while Bush was in Ireland by the sea and she was inspired by war movies she'd watched in which the hero ultimately ends up overboard.

'I love the sea,' she says. 'It's the energy that's so attractive, the fact that it's so huge. And war films where people would come off the ship and be stuck in the water with no sense of where they were or time, like sensory deprivation. It's got to be ultimately terrifying.'

The haunting and horrifying nature of the songs become distorted – try listening to the whole piece in the dark. Bush's vocal range and many textures come to the fore during the various moods and emotions of *The Ninth Wave*, which, like the sea itself, change sometimes without warning. Starting with the opening 'And Dream of Sheep' we plunge (pardon the pun) into the story as the central character is desperately trying to stay awake while floating in the water. The 'little light' is the mini-torch of the life jacket as the victim plaintively hopes for rescue while fighting against sleep, a battle that is ultimately lost and the dream sequence begins.

A cello strikes up, as someone skates across a frozen river. Then they notice something under the ice: someone is drowning under there. The whole musical track was done in a day, with the cello being produced by the Fairlight CMI.

'I mean we're talking real nightmare stuff here,' says Bush. 'At this point, they say, you know, "My god, it's me, it's me under the ice. Ahhhh!" These visitors come to wake them up, to bring them out of this dream so that they don't drown.' A long list of voices was used for the wake-up section, five of them being from the Bush family, plus those of the album mixer Brian Tench, Del Palmer and even the actor Robbie Coltrane.

'Waking the Witch' bursts forth and the conversation of a witch trial is played out over a relentless electro beat. Helicopters are sampled from Pink Floyd's *The Wall*, having originally been recorded at an airport in Los Angeles, over which is heard the command 'Get out of the water!'

'I think it's very interesting the whole concept of witch hunting and the fear of women's power,' comments Bush. 'In a way it's very sexist behaviour, and I feel that female intuition and instincts are very strong, and are still put down, really. And, in this song, this woman is being persecuted by the witch hunter and the whole jury, although she's committed no crime, and they're trying to push her under the water to see if she'll sink or float.'

The next part of the nightmare, 'Watching You Without Me', shows the victim dreaming about her friends and family at home sitting around and worrying about her absence, and watching the clock tick.

Finally a hugely uplifting passage arrives in the form of 'Jig of Life'. A glimpse into the girl's future shows that she must fight to stay alive. Written in Ireland and based on some music that Paddy Bush had unearthed, the tune is a joyous ode to staying alive. Paddy, says Kate, had 'found this piece of music and said, "You've just got to listen to this, it's brilliant. I know you'll love it!" He played it to me, and instantly I knew I wanted to use it. It was fantastic. So it was just a matter of working out a song based around the format of this piece of music he'd found. I suppose the suggestion of the fiddle as the Devil's music is not unintentional, the idea of a spirit being conjured from the future, that uncanny, uncomfortable feeling of two times meeting. And it's very much meant to be the first delivery of hope on that side of the album. There have been some very sad, disturbing experiences for the person up to this point, and although it's hardly *not* disturbing, it's meant to be a comfort. It's the future coming to the rescue of the present.'

When promoting the album, Kate discovered that talk of this track would encourage her to speak of her Irish heritage and her thoughts about the country. 'It's beautiful, totally beautiful,' she said. 'There are so many different kinds of landscapes and beauty. It's so wonderful just hanging around the coast and watching it change. It's always dramatic, stepping back into the last century. It has a real sense of magic. And the people are so fantastic, so warm, so wistful. I really do like Ireland a lot. It's one of the few places apart from England where I'd ever think of living.'

'Hello Earth' includes orchestral arrangements by Michael Kamen and a choir inspired by Warner Herzog's film version of the vampire story, *Nosferatu, Phantom der Nacht* (1979). The American composer and arranger Kamen had worked under Leonard Bernstein before forging his own fusion of rock music and orchestral pieces. In 1979 he had scored *The Wall* for Pink Floyd. 'Hello Earth' takes the victim back through the experience of the storm that put her in the water in the first place. The view is of the whole Earth and the storms can be seen dispersing away across the ocean. It was a track that Bush struggled with. '[It] was a very difficult track to write because in some ways it was too big for me. I ended up with this song that had two huge great holes in the choruses, where the drums stopped, and everything stopped, and people would say to me, "What's going to happen in these choruses?" and I hadn't got a clue. We had the whole song, it was all there, but [there were] these huge, great holes in the choruses. And I knew I wanted to put something in there, and I'd had this idea to put a vocal piece in there, that was like this traditional tune I'd heard used in the film *Nosferatu*. And, really, everything I came up with, it was rubbish, really, compared to what this piece was saying. So we did some research to find out if it was possible to use it. And it was, so that's what we did. We rerecorded the piece and I kind of made up words that sounded like what I could hear was happening on the original. And suddenly there was these beautiful voices in these chorus that had just been like two black holes. In some ways I thought of it as a lullaby for the Earth.'

With the conclusion of 'The Morning Fog' comes rescue at the dawn. Written on the Linn drum machine and with a sterling contribution from the classical guitarist John Williams, it really helps the album end on a positive note. 'It was meant to be one of those kind of "thank you and goodnight" songs,' explains Bush. 'You know, the little finale where everyone does a little dance and then they bow and then they leave the stage. I never was so pleased to finish anything in my life. There were times I never thought it would be finished. It was just such a lot of work, all of it was so much work. The lyrics, trying to piece the thing together.

'But I did love it, I did enjoy it and everyone that worked on the album was wonderful. And it was really, in some ways, the happiest I've been when I'd been writing and making an album. And I know there's a big theory that goes around that you must suffer for your art, you know: "It's not real art unless you suffer." And I don't believe this, because I think in some ways this is the most complete work that I've done, in some ways it is the best and I was the happiest that I'd been compared to making other albums.'

The cover artwork was fairly straightforward in theory but quite difficult in practice. To make it tie in with *Hounds of Love*, it was decided to use a photograph of Kate with two dogs. They wanted a portrait of Kate, because she'd been away for three years, and the dogs were obvious. Should be simple. Initial steps were taken when John Bush tried to photograph Kate with poems painted on her body in the back garden but that idea was soon shelved. 'It was very difficult trying to get a picture of myself with dogs that wouldn't look either like something out of *Country Life* or too period,' she says. 'The original idea was just to have the three heads: myself and a dog each side of me, but it just didn't work. The dogs wouldn't stay still!'

After moving into a photographic studio, they tried the approach of an overhead shot, but again the dogs were just too restless. They tried taking them for a run beforehand and then feeding them up, but still they never seemed to be sleepy. When they did settle down one of them would inevitably ruin three hours of Kate's makeup with a wayward paw.

Many hours later they managed to get the shot that was needed. For the back cover they wanted to tie in with *The Ninth Wave* and photographed Kate lying on her back in water. However, the black-and-white image used doesn't really convey this and she seems to be standing up.

The back cover also included an excerpt from a Tennyson poem. The album credited this as being from a piece called 'The Holy Grail'. It was in fact from 'The Coming of Arthur'. The embarrassing mistake was spotted by *Homeground* fanzine and corrected in the UK.

The last thing that needed to be confirmed was the age-old debate concerning which track would be the lead-off single. EMI had earmarked 'Cloudbusting' but Bush, as ever, had other ideas. It had to be 'Running Up That Hill'. She had already backed down over the title of that song, which was initially called 'Deal with God'. EMI claimed that any song with the word 'God' in the title would immediately mean that many countries (including the USA) would refuse to play it, even though the Beach Boys had success-fully released 'God Only Knows' two decades earlier. She admitted that, because of the perceived failure of *The Dreaming*, she should give the album every chance of being a success and not be so stubborn over the title of a song.

She did, however, win the argument that this song, whatever its title, should be the first single. 'I couldn't believe this,' she fumed. 'This seemed completely ridiculous to me and the title was such a part of the song's entity. I just couldn't understand it. But, nonetheless, although I was very unhappy about it, I felt unless I compromised that I was going to be cutting my own throat. I'd just spent two, three years making an album and we weren't gonna get this record played on the radio, if I was stubborn. So I felt I had to be grown up about this, so we changed it to "Running Up That Hill". But it's always something I've regretted doing, I must say. And normally I always regret any compromises that I make.'

The comeback after three years without an album reached everywhere. 'Running Up That Hill' streaked straight into the UK chart at Number 9 and was backed by copious amounts of radio airplay. This single was her first one to use the 1980s favourite single format, the 12-inch. Backed with 'Under the Ivy' it became her best-selling single since 'Wuthering Heights' seven years earlier and peaked at Number 3. BBC appearances on both *Wogan* and *Top of the Pops* no doubt helped. The latter was her first personal appearance on the show since 1978.

The video to 'Running Up That Hill' undoubtedly helped sales and was played everywhere. It had been filmed at Bray Studios by the Thames the previous April, while Bush had been working with her new dance teacher Dianne Gray. Auditions were held to find a dance partner for Kate and Michael Hervieu was given the part. He was given just one day to rehearse with Kate and then was thrown straight into three days of filming the video. He was also performing in a West End play and was fined by his union for doing both at the same time. He must also have been exhausted. The clip is one of Bush's simplest, yet most evocative, as it concentrates on the intense man–woman relationship of the song. Dressed in matching grey outfits, the two dancers put in an energetic performance in the studio lit only by two large skylights. The obligatory footage of the two running up a hill (well, along a road at least) can be forgiven.

David Munns's return to London from Canada helped ease Bush's return to public life and spurred the EMI staff into giving it their full support. 'People lost touch with her and she's an artist you have to get to know, to understand, and show her you're on her side,' said Munns on the aftermath of *The Dreaming*. 'I rang her. I went down to the farm, talked to Kate. I heard some tracks and I knew it was this wonderful record.' He convinced EMI honchos that, as she wouldn't be touring again, they should support her by allowing a large budget for filming promotional videos in lieu of the touring costs, and this was a masterstroke that allowed Bush's visual flair to flourish.

EMI also pushed the boat out for the official launch of *Hounds of Love* and hired the London Planetarium for a specially commissioned laser show to accompany the album's tracks. The assembled press were suitably impressed, but were just as eager to note that Kate and Del Palmer officially attended the premiere as a couple, arm in arm. Like many things in the Bush inner circle, the secrecy surrounding the couple's relationship was both unnecessary (everyone had known for years) and surprising (what did it matter that she was sleeping with her bass player and engineer?) – not to mention the question of why did they choose such a public display at this juncture?

The album entered the chart at Number 1, removing Madonna's *Like a Virgin* from the top spot. 'I think it's brilliant because it's the music that's done it, nothing to do with image and doing great publicity stunts,' beamed Bush. 'I've been quiet for a while and I don't feel an image can sustain that amount of time.' She was more than happy to take on the media treadmill once more. After she had granted Ireland's *Hot Press* a first interview since 1978, they wrote that she was 'the kind of artist who gives Press Officers nervous breakdowns'.

The video for the second single from *Hounds of Love*, 'Cloudbusting', was her greatest visual achievement to date. It managed to convey and reinforce the narrative of the lyric, was highly stylised and featured Donald Sutherland and a surprising-looking Kate Bush in the main parts. It was a culmination of many of

Bush's working practices as well. She'd actually been planning the visual aspects of this track as she'd been writing and recording it. 'I share the feelings of a lot of people who dislike pop videos,' said Bush at the time. 'I've discovered that, while videos are needed to go with a single, I can explore the medium of filmmaking, of what works and what doesn't.'

Bush had a strong idea that she wanted Donald Sutherland to play the part of Wilhelm Reich in the shoot while she herself would play the part of his son, Peter, from whose viewpoint the film is shot. Sutherland had played the part of the tragic father in *Don't Look Now*, one of Bush's favourite films. Initial approaches to Sutherland were through his agent and the answer was that there would be absolutely no chance of the actor's being involved, but Bush was equally adamant that he would be, so she tracked down a direct conduit to him and he said yes.

'I was really nervous,' she admitted. 'I didn't know how he would respond to me. I'm just an amateur, doing a video next to somebody of his stature. But he really helped me along and I was very happy with the video.'

Julian Doyle was recommended to direct the video on a tip-off to Kate from the film director, screenwriter and animator Terry Gilliam, and he captured the essence of the song beautifully. Bush wore her hair in a short, boyish crop, a wig handled by hairdresser-to-the-stars Anthony Yacomine. Tina Earnshaw took charge of makeup on the video shoot, having progressed through the ranks at the BBC. Today she is best known for her work on big-budget movies such as *Titanic* and *Shakespeare in Love*. The outdoor scenes were filmed in the Vale of the White Horse in Oxfordshire with the rain machine designed by associates of the renowned science-fiction artist H. R. Giger, all tubes and *Alien*-esque swirls. The final 'look' of the clip was one of a major motion picture and Bush was excited about working with such cinematic professionals.

'What's nice about the last two videos is I really feel I've worked with people who are receptive to my ideas,' she beamed. 'We actually work together. It was frustrating on some of the other videos because I felt I was going further away from what I should have been going towards.' Then, after all the hard work, *Top of the Pops* refused to show the clip, because they wanted to have Kate perform in the studio. She declined, so they vetoed the film.

In an autumn of celebration for the Bush camp the icing on the cake was probably the reception that the album received in the USA. Following on from the little bit of momentum generated by *The Dreaming*, EMI released a US mini-album in 1983, which managed to break into the *Billboard* 200. That may seem only to be a very small step in the right direction, but at least it was in the right direction. That autumn they came up with the idea of having a touring show of the *Live at Hammersmith Odeon* film in lieu of a 'real' tour. Though mainly shown at US colleges, the tour was a mild success. So, by the time of *Hounds of Love*, Bush was convinced by EMI that a North American trip was worthwhile.

After flying over on Concorde she held a packed signing session at Tower Records in Greenwich Village and gave several interviews before heading on a run of TV appearances in Canada. By Christmas, both the 'Hounds of Love' and 'Running Up That Hill' singles had reached the *Billboard* Top 30, her best US chart showings to date, and the album peaked at Number 30 on the *Billboard* chart.

Against all the odds, she had not only recaptured the public's imagination and been regaled with the critics' praise, but had even surpassed her own high standards. This was to be the high point of her career, and she'd done it all on her own terms and in her own time. The only question that now remained was, where could she go from here?

Chapter Eleven

We Communicated Emotionally

London, Kent and Bulgaria, 1986–90

'They didn't speak a word of English and we didn't speak any Bulgarian, but we could communicate through music, so that absolutely transcended barriers. There were things we needed to translate but, generally, we communicated emotionally, and I just loved that. They'll come up and give you a big cuddle. They'll just come up and touch you and cuddle you, and you can go up and give them a big cuddle, and I really enjoyed that kind of communication. It felt very real and direct to me. I'd never experienced that kind of communication before. It's something we could do with more of. It's a lovely thing.'

KATE BUSH

FOR KATE BUSH THIS WAS really a flight into the unknown. Apart from her brief tour in 1979, she had rarely visited Europe, aside from brief promotional jaunts to France, West Germany, Holland and Italy, and she had certainly not travelled as far east as Bulgaria. Now, though, almost a decade later, she and her entourage had just flown into Sofia airport and were being driven across the capital. Outside, through the rain, they glimpsed symbols and monuments to the communist regime that would fall in just a matter of months. Their destination was a recording studio, where they were met by arranger and interpreter Dimitr Penev, a not uncommon name in Bulgaria, though no one was sure whether this was the man who had kept goal for the 1970 Bulgarian World Cup team. The purpose of the trip was to meet up with the Trio Bulgarka, an unusual ethnic vocal trio whom Bush was going to try to persuade to follow her back to England and work on her next album.

★   ★   ★

EMI were well aware that, though *Hounds of Love* had been a massive success, they might not get another Kate Bush album to market for several years. In the meantime, she won the *Record Mirror* Album of the Year and Single of the Year awards (for 'Running Up That Hill') and she was voted the *Sounds* Female Vocalist of the Year. At the Brit Awards she was nominated in three categories but failed to capture any of them, with Annie Lennox pipping her to the Best Female award.

Not wanting to lose any momentum, EMI tentatively floated the idea of a greatest-hits package. After all, she was riding her biggest commercial wave since 1978–79. Before that, though, they decided to get as much mileage as they could from *Hounds of Love* and issued two further singles: the album's title track and 'The Big Sky'. For the former she made another appearance on *Top of the Pops* and for the latter she enlisted the co-operation of around a hundred fans to appear as extras in the promotional video. The Bush-directed 'Hounds of Love' video was filmed over Christmas 1985 and was inspired by *The Thirty-Nine Steps* at the suggestion of Paddy. Look out for 'cameos' by Alfred Hitchcock and Albert Einstein in the clip.

In February and March the 'Hounds of Love' single reached the Top 20 while the likes of Billy Ocean's 'When the Going Gets

Tough' and soul diva Diana Ross's 'Chain Reaction' topped the charts. The fluidity of the UK charts was shown in its full glory as, by the time 'The Big Sky' stalled just inside the Top 40, *Spitting Image* had taken the top spot with 'The Chicken Song' at the height of their satirical take on Thatcherism.

Through the mid-1980s, large-scale celebrity-endorsed charity events were becoming commonplace in the UK. The Prince's Trust, for which Kate had performed, had run for years and the Children in Need appeal was now an annual fixture on our screens. But it was the spectacular Live Aid concerts that pushed things even further and spawned a trail of other events such as Sport Aid and Comic Relief, both of which would benefit by Kate's involvement.

During 1986 Bush was more visible than ever before in supporting charitable causes. First she sang at a Comic Relief fundraiser ('Breathing' and then 'Do Bears . . .?' in a memorable duet with Rowan Atkinson); later in the year she helped launch the official Comic Relief book; then she took part in Sport Aid's mini-marathon alongside a host of other celebrities.

During the year she sang on Peter Gabriel's song 'Don't Give Up' for his mainstream breakthrough album *So*. 'Kate did a great job,' says Gabriel. 'I'm a great fan of her singing and her voice. I think she sang that track differently to how she sings on her own records, in a very sensitive way. There are similarities in the way we work. She works as slowly as I do, which is reassuring.' When released as a single in the autumn it reached the Top 10 alongside aural atrocities such as Nick Berry's 'Every Loser Wins' and Europe's 'The Final Countdown'. She also sang on the album of the Scot rockers Big Country, *The Seer*, giving a typically ethereal vocal performance.

In the summer, *Sounds* put her on its cover. After lengthy attempts to get an interview failed, they chopped her up instead, taking swings at her 'wealthy middle-class' upbringing and constantly referring to her output as art rock, which in the writer's mind seemed to be a bad thing. They're probably Franz Ferdinand fans now. Around the same time John Bush self-published a book of his photographs documenting Kate's early years. Titled simply *Cathy*, it was planned to be the first of a trio of books, but production problems and second thoughts over his sister's privacy meant the intended second and third volumes were scrapped.

With David Munns pulling the strings at EMI, Kate was enjoying her best relationship with the label since the very early days with Bob Mercer. 'This is my favourite artist in the world,' said Munns. 'But for someone like her it's sometimes a lonely road and that can be difficult for people to understand. Make a record that's a bit obscure and some people in the company may start to say things to the artist that aren't sensible. Well, EMI and Kate just lost the plot for a while.'

But, even though things were going swimmingly, when Munns suggested a 'best of' compilation, Bush was reluctant to give her OK. But Munns could talk a good talk. It would buy her time between albums, he, argued and commercially it was the best time since 1978 to 'cash in'; also, it would draw together early fans who had dropped out around *The Dreaming* and the new ones who had become fans with *Hounds of Love*. Best of all, from her point of view, he guaranteed that she would have to do very little promotion for the collection, since EMI would mount a massive press and TV advertising campaign. They would want a new song to be included, but they offered a big video-filming budget to go along with it, something that was very attractive to the cinematic aspirations of the singer.

Bush relented and agreed to the project, but she wanted it to be done in a 'tasteful' way and set about designing a cover with brother John. Together they came up with a simple black-and-white portrait (not a million miles away from the Mankowitz shots that had been used on *Lionheart*) for the album, to be called *The Whole Story*. The rear showed a still from the 'Cloudbusting' video. As well as working on a new song, Kate wanted some changes to the older material going on the album. 'Wow' was remixed and for 'Wuthering Heights' she insisted that she redo the vocal.

She was getting quite a reputation for being demanding to the point of obsession over the finer points of her new work, but going back to rerecord songs almost a decade old was taking things a bit far. Surely it was a record of her as a 19-year-old. Why start again? 'I'm happy with my voice now,' she said. 'I suppose I wanted to make "Wuthering Heights" somehow step up through the decade. It sounded very dated to me: my voice sounded so young; the production sounded so 1970s. I like the idea of taking the song I'm most associated with, and making it me now as opposed to a very young girl, as I was in 1977.'

The new song she offered for the album was the epic 'Experiment IV'. Telling the story of a military sound experiment (with Nigel Kennedy playing violin) that could cause a 'sound spirit' to kill was perfect for a big-budget narrative video shoot. Kate decided to direct the clip herself and appears only briefly, but she added the talents of a host of TV stars to the cast. Dawn French and Hugh Laurie were among the high-profile cast members who took part. It was filmed in a disused southeast London military hospital, where she managed to get a full-scale movie feel to the proceedings. Kate 'appears' in the clip as the demon in a startling facemask designed by Charles Knode, who was known for his work on numerous movies, including *Jabberwocky, Life of Brian, Blade Runner* and *Never Say Never Again*.

The Whole Story was a smash, going straight to Number 1 and selling more than a million copies. The accompanying video collection also topped the charts. This included the same 12 songs as the album did, though the video for 'Wow' was removed and replaced by a live-clips montage to the song. Kate attended a party for fans jointly held by the Kate Bush Fan Club and *Homeground* fanzine to celebrate the compilation's success.

In February 1987, no doubt helped by *The Whole Story*, she won the Best Female Singer award at the Brits and in March she joined

David Gilmour to sing at two *Secret Policeman's Third Ball* concerts for Amnesty International. They performed 'Running Up That Hill' and 'Let It Be'.

For the next two years Bush was mostly a figure back in the shadows of the UK pop industry. She made a couple more charity appearances and, according to a story in the *Guardian* on 1 April 1988, was set to join the cast of *Doctor Who*.

Over the summer of 1988 news began to leak out that Bush had been working with – wait for it – a Bulgarian folk trio called the Trio Bulgarka. That autumn, the *NME* carried an extensive interview about these interesting sessions. Paddy Bush had originally become interested in the Bulgarian folk scene and had played Kate a tape of some music at the end of the *Hounds of Love* sessions. 'It was the most incredible thing I've ever heard, beautiful,' says Bush. 'So I decided I wanted to work with them in some form in the future. But it takes me a long time to digest ideas. Even if I read a book it maybe won't come out into a song until four years later. So I wrote a track with a choir-synthesiser sound hoping that, if we could get to work with them, they would take the weight of the song from the synthesisers.'

After writing much of the new album, Bush made contact with the trio through their UK producer, the legendary Joe Boyd (of Nick Drake, Richard Thompson and Fairport Convention fame). It was arranged for Kate to fly out to Bulgaria to meet the trio and, if everything went well, they'd return to London to sing on the album. 'I was very worried because chances were it might not work,' says Bush. 'It might just sound like we'd bunged them in a Western track. I really didn't want them to be dragged down to my level. I was worried that they wouldn't want to get involved with Western pop music, because it has a bad name and a lot of people are initially scared of it. I don't blame them at all.'

Bush spent three days rehearsing with the trio of Yanka Rupkina, Eva Georgieva and Stoyanka Boneva, in the presence of an interpreter, since neither side could utter a word of the other's language. 'Kate's very popular in Bulgaria,' said Yanka Rupkina. 'Young people like her very much. She sings emotionally. There's lots of lovely thinking in her writing and she's a very good musician. It is our first time with such a famous singer, and we hope we'll work with her in the future, if we haven't caused her too many worries.'

The trio managed to produce heartfelt, powerful music, even if you couldn't understand a word of what was being sung and no matter what the subject matter. Dimitr Penev was drafted in as arranger for the sessions, because he had a special understanding of the traditional arrangements they wanted to employ. 'You're not distracted by words,' said Bush. 'All you're picking up are the emotions that they're translating to you. It feels like very deep information. There's one point when Yanka's belting it out, really fantastic, yet she's singing something like, "Marco sits down with his mother and has some bread and jam"!

'I've been so excited doing it and it's so lovely for me to work with women as well, a tremendous difference. And, because we can't talk intellectually, we can't talk about the state of Bulgaria or even what the shops are like in London; our whole communication is totally emotional.'

The writing for the album had progressed as it had for the previous two albums. Kate would work on demos and ideas at the home studio with Del Palmer engineering. The composition tool of choice was still the Fairlight CMI and, as with *Hounds of Love*, they used what might be called demo recordings to start as a base and built layers on top of the original sounds. 'Most of the time it's just the two of us in there,' said Bush about her close working relationship with Del Palmer. 'He works a lot on the rhythms and things, so at least I'm not totally alone in there. Once the song feels good enough to work on, then you bring musicians in and just sort of layer upon layer. You sort of create the picture, as it were, and just build up the sounds that seem to work for what the song is saying. It feels as though songs have personalities. You can try something on a song and it will just reject it. It doesn't want it. And yet you can try that on another song and it will work so perfectly. They're all so individual.'

When the initial sounds had been achieved she started to bring in the musicians, often one at a time, to add their parts to the process. Drummer Stuart Elliott kept up his record of playing on every Kate Bush album. 'I think it's good to keep that long-term relationship,' Kate said at the time. 'He's so easy to work with because he knows what I'm like. Occasionally I even ask him to use cymbals on a track now! He's been through that whole stage where I just couldn't handle cymbals or hi-hats. Now that I'm actually using them again, he can't cope.'

The players Kate used on the album were a wide-ranging bunch: Nigel Kennedy played on a couple of songs; her father recorded a spoken-word part for another; Eberhard Weber was one of four bassists; Charlie Morgan also drummed; and Dave Gilmour added his guitar playing expertise to 'Love and Anger'.

The album was titled *The Sensual World* and took in influences and sounds from across the globe. Sessions were held in Dublin's Windmill Lane Studios again, where Donal Lunny, Davey Spillane and John Sheahan added their unique Celtic flavourings to the proceedings. The U2 and Elvis Costello associate Kevin Killen was also involved. Bush met Killen while working with Peter Gabriel and he was given the task of mixing the finished album.

The three songs with the Trio Bulgarka were recorded at London's Angel Studios in October 1988 and parts of these sessions were filmed by the BBC for their *Rhythms of the World* series. On the show, Eva Georgieva, speaking through a translator, said, 'Music does not recognise the existence of two systems. Music travels around the world without a visa, without a passport. Music is international. The opportunity our trio had to record with Kate Bush was very important to us and we consider it a great honour. I think that everything went well. We coped well with the variety of rhythms and our composer Dimitr Penev was a great help. I think that Kate Bush was satisfied with the work we did together. I think she chose to work with Trio Bulgarka because we are folk singers with strong musical roots and able to meet any musical challenge we are faced with.'

Many fans were not overly impressed with *The Sensual World*, especially the fact that it took four years to arrive. It included several mid-paced, middle-of-the-road tracks that failed to sparkle. Musically, the let-down was a shame, because many of the sentiments she tried to convey were intensely personal and emotional. Casual observers could be forgiven if they didn't believe that this was the person who had produced *Hounds of Love*. In interviews Bush explained that she felt this to be her most personal and most honest album.

'And I think it's my most feminine album,' she added. 'I feel maybe I'm not trying to prove something in terms of a woman in a man's world. On *The Dreaming* and *Hounds of Love*, particularly from a production standpoint, I wanted to get a lot more weight and power, which I felt was a very male attitude. In some cases it worked very well, but this time I felt braver as a woman, not trying to do the things that men do in music.'

One of the album's best tracks was the opening one, 'The Sensual World'. Church bells ring out as Bush uses Molly Bloom's speech at the end of James Joyce's *Ulysses*. In the speech she talks of the time she was proposed to and so the image of church bells announcing a wedding fell into place. Bush wanted to use the speech as the lyric to the song but was refused permission. So she had to sit down and write her own words. She also had to rewrite parts of the instrumentation. 'I had a rhythm idea with a synth line I took home to work on one night,' she said. 'While I was playing it, this repeated "Yes" came to me and made me think of Molly Bloom's speech right at the end of *Ulysses*. I went downstairs and read it again, this unending sentence punctuated with *yeses* – fantastic stuff. And it was uncanny: it fitted the rhythm of my song.' Bush decided to rewrite the song as being about the

Bloom character, about her leaving the printed page and stepping into the sensual world. 'I tried to write it like Joyce,' she laughs. 'The rhythm at least I wanted to keep. Obviously I couldn't do his style. It became a song about Molly Bloom, the character, stepping out of the page and into the real world, the sensual world. Touching things. The grass underfoot! The mountain air! I know it sounds corny, but it's about the whole sensual experience, this wonderfully human thing.'

The Celtic trio of Lunny, Spillane and Sheahan work perfectly with the track, giving a sense of wonderment and discovery, even if you don't know the background to the song.

'Love and Anger', with its irrepressible rhythms, was one of the most difficult to finish. Bush admitted to taking over a year and half before she had it nailed down. Dave Gilmour's guitar gives the song great strength during the chorus. The lyric is one of Bush's longest, but she wasn't sure where it was going. 'I just couldn't get any lyrics or work out what to do with the instruments,' she admitted. 'I just didn't know what I wanted to say. Really, it was a bugger, that song. And in some ways I still don't know what I'm wanting to say. If I'm saying anything, it's that if people are having a hard time and things look really dark, and it seems like you can't get out, then try not to worry too much. It'll be all right – someone will come and help.'

'The Fog' was one of two consecutive songs addressing parent–child relationships. Kate's father speaks the opening dialogue with Kate. 'I started with the idea of a relationship in deep water and thought I could parallel that with learning to swim, the moment of letting go,' she says. 'When my dad was teaching me to swim he'd hold both my hands, then say, "Now, let go." So I would. Then he'd take two paces back and say, "Right, swim to me." I thought it was such a beautiful image of the father and child, all wrapped up in the idea of really loving someone, but letting them go, because that's a part of real love, the letting go.'

Michael Kamen arranged the strings and Nigel Kennedy provided the solo violin. 'He's great to work with, such a great musician,' says Bush of the violinist. 'The times we work together we sort of write together. I'll say something like, "What about doing something a bit like Vaughan Williams?" and he'll know the whole repertoire. He'll pick something, and maybe I'll change something. By doing that we came up with this different musical section that hadn't been on the Fairlight.'

Sounds of waves and seagulls wash over the later sections. It is a very touching and emotional piece of music that was clearly very personal to the singer.

The fourth track, 'Reaching Out', looked at the mother–child relationship and quite simply how the child reaches out for her. 'That was really quick, really straightforward,' Kate said of the track. 'A walk in the park did that one for me. I really needed one more song to kind of lift the album. I was a bit worried that it was all sort of dark and down. I'd been getting into walks at that time, and just came back and sat at the piano and wrote it, words and all.' The song was certainly uplifted by the strings, arranged again by Michael Kamen.

'Head's We're Dancing' was one of the most talked-about songs on the album, but also one of weakest. The basic premise was that a woman meets a man at a party and, not knowing who he is, accepts the invitation to dance. Later she finds out that the dashing charmer was actually Adolf Hitler. Musically, the track never really gets going, its herky-jerky rhythm is swamped by all manner of things that distort the whole song. Bush's vocals are washed away and the whole thing sounds as if a good few 'layers' should have been removed.

Mick Karn, the bass player for Japan, played on this track, though most of his work is hard to decipher. 'He came along with a part that he'd worked out,' she said. 'I'd sent him a cassette. It was fabulous. He understood the whole storyline. I hadn't sent any lyrics or anything, and he just kind of played this part. It was so right for the song. I was really knocked out. He's a very nice person as well as a great musician.'

'Deeper Understanding' addressed Bush's electronic obsessions for the first time. The character in the song sings about having just the black box of a computer for a friend. Though the song is not directly autobiographical, she must have experienced some of the feelings expressed in the song at some point, especially during the harder parts of working on the album with just a Fairlight CMI for company. Though the track was almost complete by the time the Trio Bulgarka came on the scene, Bush came up with the idea of using their distinctive vocals to act as the computer talking back to the singer. 'I wanted this sound that would almost be like the voice of angels, something very ethereal, something deeply religious, rather than a mechanical thing,' says Bush. 'We went through so many different processes, trying vocoders, lots of ways of affecting the voice, and eventually it led to the Trio Bulgarka. It made absolute sense because they have a certain quality. Their music feels so old and deep. I think it is like the voice of angels.'

'Between a Man and a Woman' is about a third party coming, as the title suggests, between a man and a woman. Musically pedestrian, it doesn't really go anywhere, though the combination of Alan Murphy's guitar and Jonathan Williams's cello works well together. But, generally, it's what the fast-forward button was invented for! 'Never Be Mine', likewise, is mid-paced and, despite the myriad influences provided from Ireland, Germany and Bulgaria, it's a forgettable track.

'Rocket's Tail' was written specifically for the Trio Bulgarka and their vocals rise and sail about with Bush's passionate voice twisting between and around them. It's an excellent song that threatens to save the ending of the album and is really something quite different for Kate Bush. The song is sung *a cappella* until the band kicks in over halfway through, and the thing drops down a notch or two.

'We took it to Bulgaria and started working with this arranger,' Bush said. 'I told him what I wanted, and he just went off and said, "What about this?" And they were great. He kept giving me all these things to choose from, and we worked so well together. It was so good that we decided to hold the drum kit – it was originally starting much earlier in the song. Then we let Dave Gilmour rip on it, so we'd have this really extreme change from just vocals to this hopefully big rock'n'roll kit, with bass, and guitar solos.' Well, she achieved what she wanted – it just didn't work that well.

'This Woman's Work' (written for the John Hughes film *She's Having a Baby*) is a beautiful ending (for the vinyl version of the album, at any rate). 'That was a really easy song to put together,' she explained. 'All that was added to the piano was a bit of Fairlight, a bit of backing vocals and a tiny amount of orchestra, about four or five bars. But the difference it makes is extraordinary.'

The simplicity of the song makes it stand out from much of the rest of the album. This breath of fresh air is infuriating because a little more restraint on some of the earlier tracks could have made this a really classic album instead of just an OK one.

'Walk Straight Down the Middle' was added to the CD and cassette versions of the album. With amazing understatement, Bush said of this track, 'I wrote the lyrics, recorded the vocals, backing vocals and synth overdubs in one day, which is totally unheard of for me.' She did go back the next day and add more layers, though, before mixing. Still, it was amazingly quick. For a quickly recorded 'bonus' track it isn't bad, but it's too close to some of the self-indulgent earlier songs to be a great ending. Vinyl listeners probably had it better by going out with the ending of 'This Woman's Work'.

As usual, the cover photograph was taken by John Bush, again a close-up portrait of Kate, this time holding a large flower in front of her mouth. The album's release put Kate in the most out-of-kilter position compared with the rest of the charts since 'Wuthering Heights' was thrust into the cauldron of punk and disco. Now it was the extremes of manufactured Stock–Aitken–Waterman drivel or the burgeoning Manchester indie-dance crossover sounds that were everywhere you cared to listen. How would a thirtysome-thing female singer-songwriter backed by a Bulgarian folk trio fit in – even though the former Talking Heads frontman David Byrne had been championing world music with his new album the same year?

The single 'The Sensual World' was released in mid-September, reaching Number 12 in the UK, and the album followed a month later. In the US her new label, Columbia, decided it was best to release 'Love and Anger' instead. An EMI marketing ploy had come up with the idea to double-track the 12-inch single version of 'The Sensual World'. It meant that one side of the record had two different grooves etched in, which would play either the single or the instrumental mix. While not exactly rocket science, this foxed many buyers into thinking they'd bought a dodgy record. BLEAT ABOUT THE BUSH, declared the *Daily Mirror*, which reported that 'Record dealers are furious with Kate Bush because they're facing hordes of youngsters who reckon they've been sold faulty copies of her new 12-inch single.' It was reissued with an explanation sticker on the cover.

The follow-up singles, 'This Woman's Work' and 'Love and Anger', suffered through too little airplay – being seen as out of touch with the singles charts of the day – and reached Numbers 25 and 38 respectively in the charts. For her own part, Bush gave only a few interviews and refrained from making any in-store appearances, though she did fly to the US for a short promotional visit.

Though she didn't release any new music in 1990, aside from some B-sides, she was in the news. In the Sunday tabloid *People*'s supplement she was famously photographed being restrained by Del Palmer while wagging an angry and accusing finger at the paparazzi. In an attempt both to pacify and to control the media image of herself, she took the unusual step of inviting the *Daily Mirror* to visit her at her home. Presumably, opening herself up in a controlled manner would calm the need for more press intrusion and allow her to reveal what she wanted and keep private the rest. In the event, the article didn't really say anything new to even the most casual fan. She lives in a 'modest' house, owns cats, likes to cook and says, 'You can hardly call me a recluse because I stay in and watch telly a lot.'

In March 1990 the BBC screened the *Comic Strip* film *Les Dogs*, in which Kate played the bride. She also wrote some music for the series, including the soundtrack to the episode entitled *GLC* and the song 'Ken'.

In 1988, EMI had taken the unusual step of contacting a fanzine (*Homeground*) about how it should best transfer Kate's back catalogue to CD. Co-editor, David Cross, had been involved with the record industry for some time and later worked for EMI. The label wanted *Homeground* to canvass opinion as to whether it was better to put out extra tracks on CDs, or maybe a single- or double-disc set of B-sides. It was a strange thing to ask, because whatever feedback they did get most likely didn't include a high-priced box set of all her albums, which included two discs of extra tracks into the bargain. Most fans would surely just want the extras. But that's how the *This Woman's Work* box set was issued in 1990.

After a three-year gap between *The Dreaming* and *Hounds of Love*, and then a four-year gap between that album and *The Sensual World*, fans were left to speculate on when Kate Bush would be seen again. After more than a decade, most had given up hope of seeing a live tour ever again. Bush again slipped away to her own life. Living happily with Del Palmer, and, with brother John and his family living next door, she was enjoying her privacy.

'When I took that break from *The Sensual World* I really got into gardening,' she revealed. 'It's literally a very down-to-earth thing, isn't it? Real air. Away from the artificial light. Very therapeutic. I've never had a garden before, just very down-to-earth things like that. Again, it's just having a bit of contact with nature, and planting things and seeing the slowness of it all. I've planted a flower bed; you have to be very patient. And it's a good thing for me to work with, because making an album, you have to be very patient, and this flower bed helped me, tremendously, to watch how things have to fight for space. You have to get the weeds out, a little bit of water every day, every day a little something.'

Chapter Twelve

Achieve Something That Is Quite Imperfect

London, 1991–94

'I really don't think that it's possible to make things perfect,
really. In some ways, there's almost an attempt to try to
achieve something that is quite imperfect. Do you know
what I mean? And to be able to find a way of leaving it
with certain raw edges, so that the heart doesn't go out
of it. I don't think of myself as a perfectionist at all.'

KATE BUSH

PRINCE ROGERS NELSON, formerly known as Prince, and
at the time of this studio session known simply by his
'symbol', had just received the tapes from England. He was
about to embark on one of the most unlikely collaborations of
his long and illustrious career. Unable to meet up in person with
the writer of this song, he had been sent the master tapes with
some notes about what might be required. He immediately set
about adding the full range of his talents to the song. In truth he
probably went over the top and added too much. Then he sent
the result back to Kate Bush, but she and her associates didn't
quite know what to make of them.

★　★　★

At the end of 1990 one of the most popular Kate Bush conventions ever was held at the Hammersmith Palais in London with 1,200 attendees. The highlight of the day was a 45-minute Q&A session that Kate held from the stage, when she casually let slip that she was planning to play some live shows in 1991! It wouldn't be a full tour, but some whole concerts for the first time in 12 years. Everyone present, including the EMI representative, was gob-smacked. After 12 years of waiting would she really being playing live? Excitement grew when the *Homeground* fanzine reported that Kate had bought two more Fairlights 'for touring purposes'. But 1991 came and went, and then, on Valentine's Day in 1992, Kate's mother Hannah died at the age of 72.

For such a close family it was a devastating blow. All thoughts of recording and tours were dropped completely and Kate withdrew to deal with her grief. 'I haven't been able to write about any of it. Nevertheless, the experience is in there,' said Kate much later. 'It's something I couldn't possibly express in music, and yet it is being expressed through very subliminal things, like the quality of some of the performances. I couldn't work for months; I couldn't go near the whole process. I had no desire to start, no desire to work at all. It was a terrible shock for all of us. Really, I'm so grate-ful that we had so much time together and we had such a good relationship. I had an incredibly good relationship with her, as I did all my family.'

Kate had already had to deal with other grief during the early 1990s. At the aforementioned convention there had been dedica-tions to the memories of both guitarist Alan Murphy and dancer Gary Hurst. Long-time dance partner Hurst died after battling an AIDS-related illness while Murphy's loss as a studio collaborator also hit her. His last contribution had been to *The Sensual World*. He had also played with Level 42 and Go West.

'He was a guitarist who I felt used his instrument like a voice,' said Bush. 'But also like a chameleon, I guess. He could just change it into anything. "Al, I want you to be a racing car." Fine, he'd become a racing car. "Al, could you be this big panther creeping through the jungle." You could throw any imagery at him and he would never balk, he would just be with you, you know. Making albums will never be the same again for me without Alan. I'll miss him terribly. I already do, as a person as well as a musician.'

The recording of Kate's seventh album had started in 1991 and restarted in late 1992 after Hannah's death that previous February. It would finally be released in 1993, four years after *The Sensual World*, a length of time comparable to the previous gap. Considering the interruption caused by Hannah's death, it was actually quite a quick turnaround for Kate. She had started the recording process with great hopes of finishing the album in a relatively short time, but once she was at work in the studio it went out of her hands.

'It's ridiculous, isn't it?' she mused. 'Three years to make a record. The worst [thing] is the stuff is often written very quickly. A day, a day and a half, but once you get into the studio it starts to take on a life of its own. But I wouldn't understand it if I wasn't involved. I'd think it was outrageous.'

The sessions were a case of something old, something new. The old was the now favoured method of early demos with Del, composing on the Fairlight and keeping the original demos as a base, then adding layers on top. The new was a list of new collaborators who were invited to join in. As with *The Sensual World*, almost all of the album was written in the studio. Del Palmer also stepped forward to talk to the press for the first time in any depth. 'There's no fixed method to how Kate works,' he explained, 'but, generally speaking she will say, "Can you get me a drum pattern that sounds like this?" She'll sing me something and I'll program the Fairlight with a simple eight-bar loop, never any more than that, and then she'll program a sound in the Fairlight and get a tune going. Then she'll say, "I've got something, can I put a vocal down?"

'If Kate's singing really loud she backs off from the mike and then she comes right in close for the quiet stuff, but when she breathes in she does this to the side. I have to say that, from a purely technical standpoint, it's really badly done – there's just so much compression on everything. But I'm not interested in being technical. I just want it to sound good, and, if it does, then what's the point of changing it?'

The Trio Bulgarka again contributed to three songs; Stuart Elliott and John Giblin re-formed as the rhythm section that had operated on *The Sensual World*; and the major new addition to the core band was Danny McIntosh, who replaced Alan Murphy on guitar. McIntosh had been a member of the blues rockers Bandit in the late 1970s, when they released two albums (*Bandit* in 1977 and *Partners in Crime* the following year).

The star guests were diverse and in some cases unusual. They were invited on a song-by-song basis but overall it tended to give a disjointed feel to the album as a whole. Colin Lloyd-Tucker sang on a couple of songs while Gary Brooker played Hammond organ on a couple of others. Nigel Kennedy appeared again; Lenny Henry, Jeff Beck, Prince and Eric Clapton all appeared on a song each.

With the original idea being to record quickly and take the album on the road, it isn't surprising that the recording process had a little more of a live feel to it than any of Kate's albums stretching back to *The Dreaming*. Many tracks featured Stuart Elliott (drums) and John Giblin (bass) playing at the same time. Del Palmer took a step out of the studio and into the control room, because he wanted to concentrate on the engineering and didn't want to play in any live band that might go on tour, though of course that never materialised.

The Red Shoes opened with 'Rubberband Girl'. It was possibly the most upbeat pop song she'd ever written and scored well in the charts, reaching Number 12. It could have been a mid-period Prince song (though he had nothing to do with it), such was the discernible tighter performance of the band. 'On "Rubberband

Girl" the bass, drums and basic keyboards were all done together,' explained Del Palmer. 'We did change the whole track afterwards in the sense of editing it digitally rather than redoing tracks. The bass and drum sound was important because we wanted to have them consistent throughout the album.'

The song infectiously bounces along and sounds like a basic rock song. The new approach (or the return to the old approach, depending on which way you look at it) certainly gave the album a promising start. The horn section was also a rarely used tool in the Bush repertoire and gave the track a hint of the Stax sound. 'When you put later tracks down, the earlier ones sometimes have to change because the whole feel of the piece changes,' said Palmer. 'Sometimes we had to do the bass and drums three or four times, not because we were unhappy with the original performances, but because the feel of the song had altered as new tracks were added. "Rubberband Girl" is one of the few that worked first time.'

'And So Is Love' slowed things right down. Continuing the theme of looking forward to live performances of the songs, the Fairlight was cut wherever possible after the original demos were completed. Gary Brooker's Hammond organ lays a comfortable base for guest guitarist Eric Clapton's typically professional contribution. When Clapton arrived to play his part his guitar technician brought along a truck load of gear for the session. Del Palmer told Clapton that they just wanted to get Clapton's 'classic' sound. He plugged in one of his smallest amps and off he went. What made Clapton's part more poignant was that he attended the session just a couple of months after his son Conor had died when he fell 53 floors from a New York apartment window. 'I admired him for doing that,' said Del Palmer. 'He'd promised to do it and he wanted to stick to his commitment. Eric only really plays in one style, but he's a genius at what he does, so that was a highlight for me.'

'Eat the Music' takes a distinctly Caribbean vibe and then ruins it with some cod-lyrics about bananas, papaya, sultanas and so on. It probably had some sexual overtones but it was a cringeworthy song. Amazingly, it was considered to be the album's first single for a while, but, thankfully, cool heads prevailed.

'Moments of Pleasure' is the outstanding ballad of the collection, sailing just by the abyss of becoming a Celine Dion parody and passing unscathed. The tender relationship between the orchestral arrangements (provided by Michael Kamen in Abbey Road's Studio Two) and Kate's delicious piano part forms a perfect backdrop for this paean to the departed. The Douglas Fairbanks reference is directed at Michael Powell, whom Kate met in New York shortly before his death. Powell had directed the original film of *The Red Shoes* in 1948.

'I'd had a few conversations with him and I'd been dying to meet him,' recalled Bush. 'As we came out of the lift, he was standing outside with his walking stick and he was pretending to be someone like Douglas Fairbanks. He was completely adorable and just the most beautiful spirit, and it was a very profound experience for me. It had quite an inspirational effect on a couple of the songs.' Other friends who are included are 'Smurf', a reference to the departed Alan Murphy, Gary Hurst (Bubba), John Barrett (Teddy), Bill Duffield (Bill). Kate's mother and aunt Maureen are also mentioned.

'The Song of Solomon' uses some Bible passages with the lyric, as might be expected, given the song's title. A simple but effective track, it marked the Trio Bulgarka's first appearance on the album. From biblical to mystical.

'Lily' opens with a spoken-word section narrated by Lily herself. The Lily in question is a 'healer' whom Kate visits. The opening gives way to a funky, dare it be said almost hip-hop, beat, though it was all played live as a band piece. 'The track includes an instrument called a fujara, played by Paddy, which comes from Yugoslavia,' said Del Palmer. Bush's vocal undergoes several changes throughout the track: a yearning in the verse, a deep-voiced spoken bit in the bridge and a strong call-out during the chorus. At least one publication suggested that this song might be a thinly veiled admission that Bush was actually a white witch!

The album's title track has more than just a tinge of Irish to it. Perhaps she had her mother's old Irish dancing in mind when she wrote the up-tempo music to the track that tells the story of the shoes with a mind of their own.

'Top of the City' is an example of what had become Kate-Bush-by-numbers. A tune she could probably turn out in her sleep, but slow and plodding in places. The original Nigel Kennedy additions to the songs had been recorded way back in 1990 and, even though the track changed many times during the following years, his part remained.

'Constellation of the Heart' is the second song on the album that could have been penned by Prince – and the second one that he had nothing to do with. If this was an attempt to break into the US funk scene it failed miserably. If it wasn't such an attempt it failed anyway.

'Big Stripey Lie' is an odd beast, not really sure where it should be going. Kate played electric guitar on the track but she should probably have kept to keyboards. The song almost dies a death during her 'solo', but, unfortunately for the listener, it carries on. Apparently Danny McIntosh showed her how to play the guitar. 'It's a sort of stocking-filler track,' said Del Palmer with a straight face. '[It was] the last one to be written, and has a sort of Captain Beefheart impersonation on the bass and guitar. This one was done quite quickly by the old method of putting down one track at a time, so it's not representative of the band-orientated approach on the rest of the album.'

The Prince link-up came about when Kate went to see one of the Purple One's June 1992 shows at Earl's Court in London. He heard she was at the show and sent her a note saying how much he admired her work. Kate thought it would be great if Prince would be able to play on her new album but, as his schedule didn't allow for him to visit her in England, she sent him some tapes of a new song called 'Why Should I Love You?' for him to add some vocal parts to. As is his wont, though, he went just a little bit further than that.

'He'd looped a four-bar section from the chorus of the song that Kate had written and just smothered 48 tracks with everything you could possibly imagine,' recalled Palmer: 'guitars, keyboards, drums, voices. I sat there and thought, 'Well, this is great, but what are we going to do with it?" So, I made a general mix of the whole thing, gave it to Kate, and she puzzled over it for months. We kept going back to it over the course of a couple of years, and eventually, with a lot of editing and work on her part, she turned it back into the song that it was. We had this piece of vocal that she wanted but it was everywhere, all the way through it, so we had to take the bit that we needed and put it in where we wanted it – we had to reconstruct the verses so that they worked with her lyrics.'

Palmer took the original drums and replaced them with new recordings to match the much more upbeat song that the Prince additions had forged. One part that hadn't been done by Prince, and that Bush had asked him to do, was recorded at the last moment – by Lenny Henry! 'It was like he'd worked in studios his whole life,' said Palmer of the comedian. 'He had no trouble doing it. Kate sang him the part she wanted him to do and then he sang it. Then she asked him to do a harmony, which he worked out with her. I used a little bit of compression, just to make the voice sound a little more throaty.' Ultimately it survived to become one of the better songs on the second half of the album.

'You're the Only One' is a soul-flavoured, last-song-at-the-school-disco kind of number, saved only by the Trio Bulgarka and Gary Brooker's Hammond noodlings. Jeff Beck provided the guitar. Whether Kate put any of her own feelings directly into this song is unknown.

The Red Shoes was the first Kate Bush album not to have her face on the cover. Instead, it carried a picture of the eponymous shoes while on the back a collage of fruit (continuing the 'Eat the Music' theme) was pictured behind the track listing. The CD sleeve opened out into a poster of Kate being carried by Stewart Avon Arnold, and on the back of that was another fruit collage (this time it had all been cut open), which was overlaid with the lyrics and band listings. All photography was by John Bush as usual.

Early plays for the press included invitations to selected locations where the album was played, and numbered lyric sheets were handed out during the playback, only to be collected in again at the end. Why the secrecy over the lyrics is a mystery – they weren't even the best she'd ever written.

The album received reasonable reviews and even had a decent write-up in *Rolling Stone*, which described it as 'a solid collection of well-crafted and seductively melodic showcases for Bush's hyper cabaret style'. Not everyone agreed, though, and, it being just the second album in eight years, there was some dissension. Mysterious lyrics were mainly a thing of the past, and the Trio Bulgarka, used so effectively on *The Sensual World*, seemed to be an afterthought. If you took the best tracks from *The Sensual World* and *The Red Shoes*, you'd have a great album instead of two average ones.

One of the few television appearances Kate made was on *Aspel and Company*. The date was 20 June, which would have been her mother's birthday. She must have been sensitive to the date, and chose to sing the poignant 'Moments of Pleasure' for the show.

Overall, though, publicity for the album was pretty sparse. Interviews that Bush did consent to were often spent fending off enquiries about her personal life, something that she had battled against for 15 years now. This reluctance to open up had gained her the unofficial name of the 'Greta Garbo of Pop'.

'People ask you questions you'd only answer under psycho-analysis,' she complained. 'I think that's personal and I'm here to talk about my work,' she told the *Sunday Times*. 'My private life, I don't want to let go of. I need to keep it close and tender so that it's all my own.'

She did talk about her return to dancing, though, as she prepared to start work on a film. 'I've had a lot of periods off, unfortunately, because my music is so demanding and I went through a phase where I just had no desire to dance. The last couple of years, it really came back, and it's been very interesting working in an older body. Your brain seems better at dealing with certain kinds of information. And I think there's something about trying too hard which takes the dynamics out of everything. I think I've become less conscious through dancing, because it's very confrontational in a positive way, standing in front of a mirror and looking at something that basically looks like a piece of you, and you've got to do something with it.'

With her track record of successful music videos, some of which were even considered to be mini-movies, it was expected that her first full film would be great. So, having shelved the idea of doing a tour, she decided to direct and star in *The Line, the Cross & the Curve*, but things didn't turn out as well as hoped.

Her ambitious plan was to use six songs from the album ('Rubberband Girl', 'And So Is Love', 'The Red Shoes', 'Lily', 'Moments of Pleasure' and 'Eat the Music') around which to build the 45-minute film. The idea sounded good and she approached the original *Red Shoes* director Michael Powell. The original film told the story of a woman torn between her career as a dancer and the demands of her husband, who was a composer. Bush evolved this story into one in which a pair of shoes take over the wearer and dance away with her.

'He was the most charming man, so charming,' said Bush of her attempts to get Powell to work with her. 'He wanted to hear my music, so I sent him some cassettes and we exchanged letters occasionally, and I got a chance to meet him not so long before he died. He left a really strong impression on me, as much as a person as for his work. He was just one of those very special spirits, almost magical in a way. Left me with a big influence.

'There's such heart in his films. The way he portrayed women was particularly good and very interesting. His women are strong and they're treated as people.'

Without Powell, Bush set about making the film. She went back to her old tutor Lindsay Kemp for his choreography and hired Miranda Richardson to star alongside her. Richardson was well known for her roles in TV's *Blackadder*, Mike Newell's *Dance With a Stranger* and Neil Jordan's *The Crying Game*.

The film opens with 'Rubberband Girl'. In a dance studio the band are standing in a semicircle while Bush and Stewart Arnold work on an energetic dance routine that includes yo-yos and straitjackets. Inexplicably, someone then brings in a massive fan to halt the proceedings. A power failure means the band depart, leaving Bush on her own to sing 'And So Is Love' before Miranda Richardson runs in *through* the mirror. After being tricked into wearing the darned red shoes Bush is whisked through the mirror and into an unintentionally hilarious scene in which she sits on someone else's legs and begs to have the offending shoes removed. You really have to see it to believe it. Lindsay Kemp stands by some red curtains in what looks like a scene from *Twin Peaks* and then they go to visit Kate's real-life healer, Lily. She gives some advice on how to get rid of the shoes. Kate ends up in a fruit-and-veg market (sort of) for 'Eat the Music' and eventually wins the battle with Richardson.

'We were very restricted by having no money and so little time,' said Bush by way of an explanation. 'But some of it was so new to me, like working with dialogue, which I found fascinating. I really enjoyed it. The film is meant to be like a modern fairy tale. We worked on it so intensely and it's not been finished for very long, so it's really difficult for me to know what people will think of it and whether they'll get a sense of story from it. I've never done anything like this before, and it was just such an education for me. I think the most demanding thing was being in it as well as directing, and I don't think I'd do that again. I found it very difficult, just having the sheer stamina. But what a wonderful experience, and it's so different from making an album because you've got this big group of people all working together on something that has to be done quickly, and the albums are almost completely opposite to that.'

A story is there but it's weak, as is the minimal dialogue. The acting is OK and the dancing is good in patches, but as a complete experience it is quite poor – certainly one of the most disappointing things she's produced in her career. 'I shouldn't have done it,' Bush told Q magazine in 2001. 'I was so tired. I'm very pleased with four minutes of it, but I'm very disappointed with the rest. I let down people like Miranda Richardson, who worked so hard on it. I had the opportunity to do something really interesting and I completely blew it.'

In May and June 1993 *The Line, the Cross & the Curve* went out on a short tour of UCI cinemas and was presented at the 1993 London Film Festival. Other musical offerings at the festival included rap spoof *Fear of a Black Hat*, which featured 'Ice Cold', 'Tasty Taste' and 'Tone Def', Madonna in *Snake Eye* and David Byrne's *Between the Teeth*. Then it went to video and hasn't been seen since.

It was here that the story ended, sort of. Kate Bush vanished. At first we didn't know she had – it just seemed like the usual low-profile period between albums. But it went on and on. Then it seemed as if she might never come back. Things had obviously changed in her private life and her relationship with Del Palmer was at breaking point. In the late 1970s she'd been asked on her views about having children. 'I couldn't have a career and children,' she'd replied. 'It's either one or the other.' We were just about to find out which one she'd chosen.

Chapter Thirteen

There's a Few Things I'd Like to Be Doing

Away from the public eye, 1995–2005

'I don't actually worry about ageing but I am at a point when I'm older than I was and there's a few things I'd like to be doing with my life. I've spent a lot of time working and I'd like to catch up. Over the next few years I'd like to take some time off.'

KATE BUSH

THE REPORTER FROM THE NATIONAL newspaper spent a couple of days in southeast England. It seems that every couple of years a bored editor poses the question, 'Whatever happened to Kate Bush?' and a writer is dispatched to find out. This one took the usual steps of dropping in at the farm for a cup of tea with Dr Bush. He asked around the local pubs and shops for anyone who knew Kate. Did anyone know anything about her day-to-day activities away from the public eye? But, like those who had travelled this path before him, he came away pretty much none the wiser. The school of her son and the address of her house remain a mystery to the public, though he did find out that she had her groceries delivered to her house and that a member of staff collected them from the gate. To the world at large she had all but disappeared completely.

★   ★   ★

In the wake of *The Red Shoes* slipping from the charts and the disappointing critical reaction to *The Line, the Cross & the Curve*, Kate Bush took a break. Nothing unusual there: after all, she'd done that between recording her last few albums. The difference was that this break would last for a very long time. She told Q magazine,

> Life gets to you, doesn't it? I also think there's a part of me that's got fed up with working. I've worked so much that I'm starting to feel [that] I needed to re-balance, which I think I did a bit, just to get a little bit more emphasis on me and my life. The reclusive thing is because I don't go clubbing and I don't do a lot of publicity. I'm a quiet, private person who has managed to hang around for a few years. Ridiculous really. I didn't think it would be like this. All I wanted to do was make an album. That was the dream. I'd been writing songs since I was little and I just wanted to see them on an album. This was my purpose in life, to just look at the grooves and think, I did that.

It was certainly sounding as if she needed a long break, and that she wanted to live more of a 'normal' life. This wasn't necessarily an easy option, though. Because of the level of fame she'd achieved, it was never going to be likely that she'd be left alone, especially if she continued to live in the UK.

The loss of her mother and others close to her inner circle certainly seemed to have prompted a rethink about what was important in her life. She had pretty much achieved all that she could in music and the last couple of albums had shown a slight slip from the very high standards that she'd set herself throughout her career. Now seemed to be a good time to put spending time with family and friends at a higher priority.

Continuing to work certainly wasn't a financial requirement. She wouldn't have to worry about money ever again, even if she chose never to put one foot back in a studio. It was reported [Q magazine, issue 103, April 1995] that in 1992 she had paid herself the tidy sum of £130,000 and made pension contributions of a further £223,000. Three years earlier she'd put more than twice that much into her pension fund.

For someone who gave away very little about her private life, the growing realisation that she might be away from the limelight for a considerable time inevitably meant that rumours would begin. Were she and Del going to get married? Was she going to start a family? Was she an alcoholic? Had she gone mad? By the mid- to late 1990s she had all but disappeared from view, and, by much of the general public, been forgotten.

Since she'd been around for the best part of 20 years and had such a distinctive style, you could be forgiven for thinking that she would have had more of an influence on popular music, but it wasn't until well into the 1990s that her name was mentioned much by up-and-coming bands and singers. When she *was* name-checked, it was often from the unlikeliest of sources. Her ever-lengthening absence meant she started to take on more of a mythical status around the music industry.

The obvious female artists to profess a Bush influence are Björk, P. J. Harvey, Alison Goldfrapp ('There was this time during my teenage years when everyone was doing ecstasy and going out to raves, and I was at home listening to Kate Bush – on ecstasy'), Corrine from Swing Out Sister and K. D. Lang. Dusty Springfield covered 'The Man with the Child in His Eyes' (as did Hue and Cry).

The current I-love-1979 retro-mania that's crying out for the new Kate Bush album has swept along a new generation of artists, including Katie Melua and Martha Wainwright. Melua bizarrely told the *Scotsman* that she'd choose a Kate Bush song for national anthem. ' "Wuthering Heights" by Kate Bush,' she explained. 'Because the writers of the song and the book are both English heroines. I'm not sure how it would sound at sporting internationals, though.' Wainwright also sang the praises of Bush's debut single. 'I love the melody – it's really great. She does this song so well. I think anyone that can write a song this good and do it at such an early age is probably a genius.'

It isn't just the women who have been talking up the Bush factor. Outkast's Antwan 'Big Boi' Patton revealed that they were trying to get to work with Kate. He said, 'We're trying to find her, but people say she's crazy!' Patton added, 'Kate Bush's music opened my mind up. She was so bugged out, man, but I felt her. She's so f***ing dope, so underrated and off the radar.' Andy Bell from Erasure also admitted to being a Bush admirer. 'When we were doing the *Wild!* album [in 1989] we went round her house and she was so lovely and made us tea and cakes,' he revealed. 'They should rerelease her stuff. I think she's finished her next album, but she's a perfectionist, so who knows when it will come out?' Even the TV personality Davina McCall has listed 'Jig of Life' as one of her favourite songs.

With Bush gone AWOL, the music press looked for a replacement and it was Tori Amos who was unfairly saddled with the label of the 'new Kate Bush' or 'the stand-in' while Kate is away. In 1994 she spoke of first hearing about Kate. 'When I was about 17 I was playing clubs and people would come up to me and go, "You sound like Kate Bush" and at the time I would say, "I don't know that, but I've heard of her." So eventually of course I got a record and I didn't really think I sounded like her . . . we could probably do each other and nobody would know, unless you really have a good ear.'

Kate's songs have been covered by all and sundry. Tori Amos covered 'Running Up That Hill' in concert and the Divine Comedy cheekily covered 'Wuthering Heights' when playing a support slot at a Tori Amos show. The Utah Saints used a sample of 'Cloud-busting' for their 1992 hit 'Something Good' and the E-Z Posse sampled 'The Man with the Child in His Eyes'. The most successful cover of a Bush song to date is the Futureheads' 2005 take of 'Hounds of Love', which reached the UK singles chart Top 10. They said, 'We were thinking that it's a brilliant song and we thought we'd try to work it out – a little challenge. We got home and it was a really quick thing. And when we played it and it just stuck. People were going barmy for it. I think that something we try to take from Kate Bush are the arrangements of the music. She made quite melodious pop music, but it's really clever. It's not traditional verse/chorus/verse song structure. There are interesting parts coming in and out of the songs all the time.'

It's not just music. Kate has also influenced the world of fashion and design, especially now that 1980s culture is very much back in vogue as part of the rush to create 'instant nostalgia'. Sadie Frost has used 'Babooshka' at her fashion shows and designer Hussein Chalayan wrote an article for the *Independent* about Kate's influence on him:

> She was very experimental and before her time. I think that she can set an example for visual people like myself. I'm not easily impressed. But she did with music what people have done with writing. It's incredibly inventive and forward-thinking. I always wanted my work to have that level of openness.

The magazine *i-D* went even further and devoted a six-page article to Sandrine Pelletier, who had designed a Kate Bush-themed spread. The Icelandic singer Björk wrote about Kate in the same issue (which was titled THE KICK INSIDE, by the way):

> Kate Bush will always represent the age of exploring your sexuality, when you change from a girl to a woman. There were so

many records in my parents' house, so I saw a lot of album covers. I thought they were all macho and occupied with power, things I didn't like. I guess that's what I found fascinating about Kate, she totally stuck out. She was so – what's the word – so complete. The music, the lyrics and the way she looked, it all made sense. Especially for a thirteen or fourteen year old girl.

Björk was one of the female artists who had their paths to fame well oiled by the work that Bush put in a decade and a half earlier. Bush's single-mindedness and drive made it easier for female artists to express themselves without reverting to stereotypical female roles. The sometimes left-field approach changed all of that.

★　★　★

Bush's withdrawal to her home in order to grieve for her mother had almost pulled her under. As grief had become almost too much to bear, her relationship of nearly 20 years with Del Palmer had got into trouble and she slipped towards serious depression. 'I spent a lot of time sleeping and I also used to enjoy watching bad TV, like really bad quiz programmes or sitcoms. I found them fascinating,' she said. 'There had been a period, a very big period, where I hadn't grieved properly. Then work became my way of coping.'

Bush and Palmer had seemed to be inseparable throughout the 1980s, working very closely on all aspects of her career. When their romance had hit the headlines in the mid-1980s they had both commented, if only briefly, on their relationship. 'It was wonderful when I took months and months off,' she'd said about an earlier break. 'I'd cook us a vegetarian meal each evening and we had time at home to grow vegetables and watch TV together and do all the sort of nice ordinary things that I hadn't had time to do since I started making records when I was 16.'

They never seemed to have seriously considered marriage, or, if they had, they'd quickly dismissed the idea. 'We just don't need it,' said Palmer. 'We're perfectly happy exactly the way we are. I never worry about the fact that she is famous. For me there are two Kates. There is the girl at home I love and there is Kate the star. I must admit that I sometimes wonder what she sees in me but it's not something I worry about too much.' Time away from her work did little to cement her and Palmer's relationship, though, and things started to fall apart. Eventually she moved out and bought a flat in central London.

Things in Kate's private life tend to carry on and change well before news of it breaks into the media, which is really how it should be. So she'd been separated for a while from Del before news of her moving back to London made the news; and, by the time it did, she had set up home with Danny McIntosh. The two had first worked together on *The Red Shoes*. Things were brightening in her private life and she felt up to starting work on a new album in 1997. Then, just as things started to take shape, she found out she was pregnant and the couple moved into a multimillion-pound mansion in Berkshire. Their son was born in July 1998, just as Kate was turning 40. They named him Bertie.

'People say magic doesn't exist, but I look at Bertie and know it does,' said Bush. 'I'm very proud of him and I get so much joy out of being with him. It's totally incomparable with anything else. What I found very difficult since having him is finding time to talk to people because he comes first. He doesn't care whether an album comes out, so that comes second. I don't want to miss a minute of him. It's so much fun, by far the best thing I've ever done.'

Like most of her personal life the news of her child's birth was kept out of the media glare and Bertie was 18 months old before news broke that she had had a son. Then the press wanted to know everything, sending helicopters over her house to try to get a photograph. Eventually, in the summer of 2000, she was forced to put out a press release to put the record straight and explain that, just like any other mother, she wanted to spend time with her son and should be allowed to do so in private.

Unlike that of many 'celebrities', Kate's personal life has always been kept to herself, sometimes to the point of paranoia. In early interviews she worried about mentioning the name of the company she'd set up, even though it was being printed and publicised on anything related to her. In 2001 she refused to confirm or deny whether or not she and McIntosh were married. The way she refused to answer the question made it sound as if they weren't, but in the twenty-first century what does it matter? Paranoia like this makes it seem as if she has something to hide, even when she doesn't, so it's a case of ever-decreasing circles. She refuses to comment on something, so the press speculates (usually getting it wrong) and it becomes an issue, even though there isn't one there in the first place.

'I think it's impossible to move through this business – in fact, it's impossible to move through life – without adopting a bit of cynicism,' Bush says. 'It's a protective and defensive thing. People are going to rip you off, they're going to stitch you up, and if you're cynical it prepares you for the reality of this. It prepares you for things that, chances are, are going to happen to you.'

It's a real shame that a performer so loved and cherished has come to feel this way. Perhaps her worldview has been skewed beyond recognition by the immense pull of fame at such an early age. 'When we did the shows last time [in 1979],' she adds, 'I did love it. The contact with the audience was fantastic. But I did feel a tremendous sense of intensity towards me and I felt very exposed. I'm really quite a quiet, private person, and it was very difficult for me, and that's got a lot to do with why I haven't toured, which has left me without a great sense of contact with an audience. It's quite a surprise to me to think I'm a famous person. It jolts me and I think, "Oh my God!"'

Brushes with the music industry have been few over the last decade. She reportedly turned down a lifetime achievement award from the Brits because they wanted her to perform, but she did accept an Ivor Novello award and the lifetime award from Q magazine. At the latter she received a lengthy standing ovation and agreed only to be photographed with John Lydon. They made an unlikely couple but their musical paths could be traced back to their bursting out with original sounds in and around 1977.

The most surprising of her twenty-first-century appearances came when she made a shocking guest appearance to perform Pink Floyd's 'Comfortably Numb' with David Gilmour at the Royal Albert Hall. In the national press, this of course prompted speculation of a return to the concert stage on her own. But she slipped from view again. It seemed that she'd come full circle, from a hopelessly shy teenager led into the studio by Dave Gilmour to a withdrawn middle-aged mother who still felt comfortable only when he was around.

★   ★   ★

Kate Bush has now been alone for so long that most of the musicians and producers she's worked with in the past have long lost touch with her. In the late 1990s, however, Nick Launay made contact with her. 'The closest I came was when I was working with a very talented young singer-songwriter called Daniel Jones, of Silverchair, who's very underacknowledged outside Australia in my opinion,' he says. 'Like Kate, he had huge success at the young age of 14, with a song he wrote at 12, and has a very vivid imagination. When I got his new demos, I heard a song that to me sounded very "Kate Bush".

'I asked him if he had heard Kate's music. He confessed that he had never heard of her. He was after all not born when *The Dreaming* was made. I played him some of her music, and he fell in love with it. Coincidentally, he wanted a girl to sing with him on this particular song, and asked me if I thought she would sing on it. Being an optimist, I thought it was worth at least asking. To cut a long story short, I managed to send her the song via her US manager. Within a few weeks we heard back that she loved the song, and would like to sing on it! We were thrilled, as you can imagine!

'She said to send her the tape so she could do her part at her studio in England. We sent the tape off and heard back that it might take a while because she was expecting a baby. I am still very genuinely patiently looking forward to hearing what she did one day. It's nice to realise that, with artists like her, even if they are not present, they seem to be always around us, and close at all times. It's kind of like time hasn't moved on for her. I feel like I saw her yesterday.'

★   ★   ★

So what is actually known about he mythical eighth Kate Bush album? Kate had recorded demos at her home studio, which she'd upgraded for the project. Then, in 1999, she began working on the album itself. Composer Michael Kamen had added string sections to two songs. These sections were recorded with the London Metropolitan Orchestra at Abbey Road just weeks before Kamen's unexpected death in November 2003 at the age of 55. Bassist Mick Karn, who played on *The Red Shoes*, has contributed along with ever-present drummer Stuart Elliott, jazz percussionist Peter Erskine and accordion player Chris Hall. Hall emailed a French website with some news about his contribution at Bush's home studio. 'We tried Cajun accordion,' he wrote. 'But it didn't quite fit so I used a standard two row accordion in the end playing a cross between Cajun, blues and African style riffs. She seemed very excited about the album.'

Classical musicians Emma Murphy (playing recorder on a track arranged by Bill Thorpe) and Susanna Pell played on the album. One of the tracks on which the London Metropolitan Orchestra's string sessions appeared was 'How To Be Invisible', which may or may not be a comment on Kate's last 12 years.

Her break-up with Del Palmer seems to have been amicable, since he has been reported as carrying out the engineering duties on at least some of the tracks. How the album will fit into a music scene that has changed irreversibly over the decade – added to the fact that Kate has been away – will be interesting. MP3 players didn't exist in 1993, but in 2005 the *Daily Telegraph* produced a cut-out-and-keep guide to the best Kate Bush songs for downloading.

The new album and how Bush fits in with today's music scene brings us to the question of her place in musical history. Without doubt she is one of the most talented, most enigmatic, most unusual and most successful female performers of all time. The only downside seems to be a lack of humour in her work. There is a little, but you have to look pretty closely to find it. Surely no one likes everything to be taken too seriously. In the UK she is certainly one of the all-time best songwriters, and the UK has had more than a few good ones. Her effortless juxtaposing of dance, mime, film, fashion and music lets her stand alone as probably the foremost British artist of her generation. Not many people can claim that. Her passion for constant reinvention predates Madonna. Her weirdness factor elevates her above Björk. The fact that she's been able to do all of this from a feminine point of view and address subject matter that most male writers would stay a hundred miles away from is all the more rare and staggering. The relentless drive for new ideas and perfectionism from this five-foot-three woman with the cute dimples is legendary.

'I think "perfect" is . . . I have used that word in the past,' she says. 'I used it wrongly because, in a way, what you are trying to do is make something that is basically imperfect as best as you can in the time you've got with the knowledge you have. That doesn't necessarily mean "perfect", but it's to the best of my ability. I've tried to say what needed to be said through the songs, the right structure, the shape, the sounds, the vocal performance, that is, the best I could.'

She certainly did.

Picture credits

p.1 (*top*) credit unknown (*bottom*) Rex Features; p.2 (*top*) Mirrorpix, (*bottom*) Pictorial Press; p.3 Pictorial Press; p.4 © Owen Franken/CORBIS; p. 5 (*top*) Mirrorpix, (*bottom*) Pictorial Press; p. 6 (*top*) Redferns, (*bottom*) Redferns; p. 7 (*top*) Mirrorpix (*bottom*) Mirrorpix; p.8 Redferns; p.9 Redferns; p.10 Redferns; p.11 Rex Features; p.12 (*top*) Pictorial Press, (*bottom*) Rex Features; p.13 (*top*) Redferns, (*bottom*) Redferns; p.14 David C. Sheasby; p.15 Rex Features; p. 16 (*top*) Mirrorpix; (*bottom*) Rex Features

Every effort has been made to identify and acknowledge the copyright holders. Any errors or omissions will be rectified in future editions provided that written notification is made to the publishers.

Appendix A

Tour Dates/Live Appearances

1977

April to July: Various small venues, playing mainly covers with the KT Bush Band

1979

Tour of Life

2	April	Poole Arts Centre, Poole, England
3	April	The Empire, Liverpool, England
4	April	The Hippodrome, Birmingham, England
5	April	The Hippodrome, Birmingham, England
6	April	The New Theatre, Oxford, England
7	April	The Gaumont, Southampton, England
9	April	The Hippodrome, Bristol, England
10	April	The Apollo, Manchester, England
11	April	The Apollo, Manchester, England
12	April	The Empire, Sunderland, England
13	April	Usher Hall, Edinburgh, Scotland
16	April	The Palladium, London, England
17	April	The Palladium, London, England
18	April	The Palladium, London, England
19	April	The Palladium, London, England
20	April	The Palladium, London, England
24	April	Concert House, Stockholm, Sweden
26	April	Falkoneer Theater, Copenhagen, Denmark
28	April	Congress Centrum, Hamburg, West Germany
29	April	Carre Theater, Amsterdam, Holland
2	May	Leiderhalle, Stuttgart, West Germany
3	May	Circus Krone, Munich, West Germany
4	May	Guerzerich, Cologne, West Germany

6 May   Theatre des Champs-Elysées, Paris, France
8 May   Rosengarten, Mannheim, West Germany
10 May   Jahrhunderthalle, Frankfurt, West Germany
12 May   Hammersmith Odeon, London, England (Duffield benefit)
13 May   Hammersmith Odeon, London, England (filmed for video release)
14 May   Hammersmith Odeon, London, England

1986

At the following three shows Bush performed 'Breathing' and a duet of 'Do Bears . . .' with Rowan Atkinson. Each show was in aid of the Comic Relief charity.

4 April   Shaftesbury Theatre, London, England
5 April   Shaftesbury Theatre, London, England
6 April   Shaftesbury Theatre, London, England

1987

At the following two shows Bush performed 'Running Up That Hill' and 'Let It Be' with David Gilmour. Both shows were Amnesty International fundraisers under the title *The Secret Policeman's Third Ball*.

28 March   The Palladium, London, England
29 March   The Palladium, London, England

2002

At the following show Bush sang 'Comfortably Numb' with David Gilmour.

18 January The Palladium, London, England

Appendix B

Discography

'The only thing she has in common with the record business is that she makes records.'

A complete and exhaustive Kate Bush discography containing all commercial worldwide and promotional releases would easily fill a book of its own. So here is a guide to the most common and some of the most collectable issues, giving a flavour of the range of things to look out for.

SINGLES

Wuthering Heights/Kite

EMI	2719	7"	UK	1978	
EMI	8003	7"	USA	1978	
EMI	606596	7"	Brazil	1978	no picture sleeve
Sonopresse	6596	7"	France	1978	
EMI	606596	7"	Italy	1978	
Tonpress	5120	7"	Poland	1978	unique sleeve

Hammer Horror/Coffee Homeground

EMI	2887	7"	UK	1978
EMI	606877	7"	Sweden	1978
EMI	606877	7"	Italy	1978
EMR	20530	7"	Japan	1978

Them Heavy People/The Man with the Child in His Eyes

EMR	20490	7"	Japan	1978

Symphony in Blue/Full House

EMR	20567	7"	Japan	1978	

Moving/Wuthering Heights

EMR	20417	7"	Japan	1978	
EMR	20417p	7"	Japan	1978	promo

The Man with the Child in His Eyes/Moving

EMI	2806	7"	UK	1979	
Tonpress	5171	7"	Poland	1979	unique sleeve

Wow/Full House

EMI	2911	7"	UK	1979	
EMI	72803	7"	Canada	1979	gold vinyl

Breathing/The Empty Bullring

EMI	5058	7"	UK	1980	
EMI	5058p	7"	UK	1980	promo
EMI	EMS17007	7"	Japan	1980	
EMI	07286	7"	Portugal	1980	
EMI	607286	7"	Brazil	1980	promo
EMI	07286	7"	Sweden	1980	
EMI	2C00807286	7"	France	1980	

Babooshka/Ran Tan Waltz

EMI	5085	7"	UK	1980	
EMI	5085	7"	Ireland	1980	
EMI	07321	7"	France	1980	
EMI	5058	7"	Japan	1980	with lyric sheet

Army Dreamers/Delius/Passing Through Air

EMI	5106	7"	UK	1980

December Will Be Magic Again/Warm And Soothing

EMI	5121	7"	UK	1980	no picture sleeve

Sat In Your Lap/Lord of the Reedy River

EMI	5021	7"	UK	1981	
EMI	064452	7"	Spain	1981	
EMI	540	7"	Australia	1981	no picture sleeve

The Dreaming/Dreamtime

EMI	5296	7"	UK	1982
EMI	5296	7"	Ireland	1982
EMI	817	7"	Australia	1982

There Goes a Tenner/Ne T'enfuis Pas

EMI	5350	7"	UK	1982

Night Of The Swallow/Houdini

IEMI	9001	7"	Ireland	1982

Ne T'enfuis Pas/Un Baiser D'enfant

EMI	5444	7"	UK	1983
EMI	651527	7"	France	1983

Sat In Your Lap/James and the Cold Gun/Ne T'enfuis Pas/Babooshka/Suspended in Gaffa/Un Baiser D'enfant

EMI	MLP19004	12"	Canada	1983

Running Up That Hill/Under the Ivy

EMI	KB1	7"	UK	1985	
EMI	17535	7"	Japan	1985	
EMI	B8285	7"	USA	1985	
EMI	–	7"	Germany	1985	test pressing
EMI	1553	7"	Australia	1985	
EMIJ	4510	7"	South Africa	1985	

Running Up That Hill/Instrumental/Under the Ivy

EMI	12KB1	12"	UK	1985
EMI	V78651/2	12"	USA	1985

Cloudbusting/Burning Bridge

EMI	KB2	7"	UK	1985

Cloudbusting (Orgonon mix)/Burning Bridge/My Lagan Love

EMI	12KB2	12"	UK	1985
EMI	S14129	12"	Japan	1985

Cloudbusting/Cloudbusting

EMI	SPRO09995	12"	Japan	1985	promo

Cloudbusting/The Man with the Child in His Eyes

EMI	B8386	12"	USA	1985	
EMI	p-B8386	12"	USA	1985	promo

Hounds of Love/The Handsome Cabin Boy

EMI	KB3	7"	UK	1986
EMI	B8302	7"	USA	1986
EMI	B8302	7"	Canada	1986
EMI	1693	7"	Australia	1986

Hounds of Love (remix)/Jig of Life/The Handsome Cabin Boy

EMI	12KB3	12"	UK	1986

The Big Sky (single mix)/Not This Time

EMI	KB4	7"	UK	1986	
EMI	KB4	7"	UK	1986	picture disc

The Big Sky (remix)/The Morning Fog/Not This Time

EMI	12KB4	12"	UK	1986

Experiment IV/Wuthering Heights

EMI	KB5	7"	UK	1986	
EMI	EMS17676	7"	Japan	1986	promo
EMI	–	7"	Germany	1986	test pressing
EMI	1886	7"	Australia	1986	
EMIJ	2015337	7"	South Africa	1986	

Experiment IV/Experiment IV

EMI	PB8363	7"	USA	1986	promo

Experiment IV (extended)/Wuthering Heights/December Will Be Magic Again

EMI	12KB5	12"	UK	1986	

Experiment IV/Experiment IV

EMI	SPRO9892	12"	USA	1986	

Be Kind To My Mistakes

EMI	7P518705	7"	Germany	1987	promo/500 copies

This Woman's Work/Be Kind To My Mistakes

EMI	EMPD119	7"	UK	1989
EMI	2341	7"	Australia	1989

This Woman's Work (single mix)/Be Kind To My Mistakes/ I'm Still Waiting

EMI	12EM119	12"	UK	1989	

This Woman's Work

Columbia	CKS2029	CD	USA	1990	promo

The Sensual World/Walk Straight Down the Middle

EMI	EM102	7"	UK	1989	
EMI	PRP1423	7"	Japan	1989	promo

The Sensual World/Instrumental mix/Walk Straight Down the Middle

EMI	12EM102	12"	UK	1989	
EMI	CDEM102	CD	UK	1989	
EMI	12EM102	12"	UK	1989	promo

Love and Anger/Ken

EMI	134	7"	UK	1990	
EMI	EMG134	7"	UK	1990	gatefold sleeve

Rocket Man/Candle in the Wind

EMI	TRIB02	7"	UK	1991	poster sleeve
EMI	TRIBODJ2	7"	UK	1991	promo
EMI	TRIMC2	cassette	UK	1991	
EMI	PHDR50	CD	Japan	1991	3" CD

Rocket Man

EMI	TRIBODJ2	7"	UK	1991	one-sided promo

Rocket Man/Candle in the Wind/Instrumental

EMI	TRICD2	CD	UK	1991	

Rubberband Girl/Big Stripey Lie

EMI	280	7"	UK	1993	

Rubberband Girl/Rubberband Girl (ext. mix)/Big Stripey Lie

EMI	CDEM208	CD	UK	1993	
EMI	12EMPD2080	12"	UK	1993	picture disc
EMI	TOCP8014	CD	Japan	1993	promo

Rubberband Girl/Rubberband Girl (ext. mix)

Columbia	CSK5504	CD	USA	1993	promo

Rubberband Girl

EMI	CDEMDJ280	CD	UK	1993	promo/500 copies

Eat the Music/Big Stripey Lie

EMI	EM280	7"	UK	1993	withdrawn before issue – less than 20 copies survive

Eat the Music/Eat the Music (ext. mix)/You Want Alchemy/Shoedance

EMI	8814112	CD	Australia	1994	scratch'n'sniff cover

The Red Shoes/You Want Alchemy

EMI	TCEM316	cassette	UK	1994
EMI	EMI316	7"	UK	1994

The Red Shoes/You Want Alchemy/Cloudbusting (video mix)/
This Women's Work

EMI	CDEMS316	CD	UK	1994

The Red Shoes/The Red Shoes (dance mix)/The Big Sky/
Running Up That Hill (12" mix)

EMI	CDEM316	CD	UK	1994

And So Is Love/Rubberband Girl (US mix)/Eat the Music (US mix)

EMI	CDEM355	CD	UK	1994	
EMI	CDEMS355	CD	UK	1994	with 3 prints

ALBUMS

The Kick Inside

Moving/The Saxophone Song/Strange Phenomena/Kite/The Man with the Child in His Eyes/Wuthering Heights/James and the Cold Gun/Feel It/ Oh To Be In Love/L'Amour Looks Something Like You/Them Heavy People/Room for the Life/The Kick Inside

EMI	EMC3223	LP	UK	1978	
EMI	EMCP3223	LP	UK	1978	picture disc
EMI	TCEMC3223	cassette	UK	1978	
EMI	SLEM795	LP	Mexico	1978	
Capitol	SW11761	LP	Canada	1978	
EMI	EMS81042	LP	Japan	1978	
EMI	6858	LP	Argentina	1978	
Harvest	SW17003	LP	USA	1978	
EMI	CDP7460122	CD	USA	1990	long box
EMI	CDP7460122	CD	UK	1990	
EMI	EMS63026	LP	Japan	2000	

Lionheart
Symphony in Blue/In Search of Peter Pan/Wow/Don't Push Your Foot on the Heartbrake/Oh! England, My Lionheart/Fullhouse/In the Warm Room/Kashka From Baghdad/Coffee Homeground/Hammer Horror

EMI	EMA787	LP	UK	1978	
EMI	TCEMA787	cassette	UK	1978	
EMI	8582	LP	Argentina	1978	
EMI	EMS81135	LP	Japan	1978	
EMI	06406859	LP	Sweden	1978	

Never For Ever
Babooshka/Delius/Blow Away/All We Ever Look For/Egypt/The Wedding List/Violin/The Infant Kiss/Night Scented Stock/Army Dreamers/Breathing

EMI	EMA794	LP	UK	1980	
EMI	TCEMA794	cassette	UK	1980	
EMI	EMS81336	LP	Japan	1980	
EMI	EMS81336	LP	Japan	1980	promo
EMI	EMA794	LP	Israel	1980	
EMI	8934	LP	Columbia	1980	promo
EMI	8934	LP	Argentina	1980	promo
EMI	8934	LP	Argentina	1980	

Never For Ever
Selections from Delius/Blow Away/Egypt.

EMI	-	7"	UK	1980	promo

The Dreaming
Sat In Your Lap/There Goes a Tenner/Pull Out The Pin/Suspended in Gaffa/Leave It Open/The Dreaming/Night of the Swallow/All The Love/Houdini/Get Out of My House

EMI	EMC3419	LP	UK	1982
EMI	64589	LP	Italy	1982
EMI	64589	LP	France	1982
EMI	EMS91044	LP	Japan	1982

EMI	EMS91044	LP	Japan	1982	promo

The Dreaming
Selections from the album.

EMI	SPRO9847	12"	USA	1982	promo

Hounds of Love
Running Up That Hill/Hounds of Love/The Big Sky/Mother Stands for Comfort/Cloudbusting/And Dream of Sheep/Under Ice/Waking the Witch/Watching You Without Me/Jig of Life/Hello Earth/The Morning Fog

EMI	KAB1	LP	UK	1985	
EMI	EMS91113	LP	Japan	1985	promo
EMI	2403841	LP	Greece	1985	
EMI	4XT17171	cassette	Canada	1985	
EMI	4XT17171	cassette	Canada	1985	'marble' effect
EMI	ST17171	LP	Canada	1985	pink vinyl
EMI	2403841	LP	Argentina	1985	
Simply Vinyl	SVLP290	LP	UK	2001	180g

The Sensual World
The Sensual World/Love and Anger/The Fog/Reaching Out/Heads We're Dancing/Deeper Understanding/Between a Man and a Woman/Never Be Mine/Rocket's Tail/This Woman's Work/Walk Straight Down the Middle (bonus track on CD and cassette only)

EMI	EMD1010	LP	UK	1989	
Columbia	44164	LP	USA	1989	
EMI	TOCP5924	CD	Japan	1989	promo
EMI	LEMP1672	LP	Mexico	1989	
EMI	–	box set	UK	1989	includes CD album, cassettes, lyric book and biography

The Red Shoes

Rubberband Girl/And So Is Love/Eat the Music/Moments of Pleasure/The Song of Solomon/Lily/The Red Shoes/Top of the City/Constellation of the Heart/Big Stripey Lie/Why Should I Love You?/You're The One

EMI	EMD1047	LP	UK	1993	
EMI	CDEMD1047	CD	UK	1993	
EMI	–	box set	UK	1993	includes CD album, video, slides, pen, etc.
Columbia	CM53737	LP	USA	1993	
EMI	TOCP7947	CD	Japan	1993	promo

The Red Shoes

Sampler for the album includes, Eat the Music/And So Is Love/Top of the City.

EMI	CDEMDDJ	CD	UK	1993	promo

LIVE

On Stage

Them Heavy People/Don't Push Your Foot on the Heartbrake/James and the Cold Gun/L'Amour Looks Something Like You

EMI	MIMP2991	2 x 7"	UK	1979	g/fold
EMI	EMS10001	12"	Japan	1979	
Sonopresse	PM211	12"	France	1979	
EMI	ED36	12"	Australia	1979	
Harvest	DLP3005	12"	Canada	1979	

COMPILATIONS

The Single File

Thirteen x 7" singles covering 1978 to 1983 inclusive.

EMI	KBS1	box set	UK	1983

Singles included:

Wuthering Heights/Kite	EMI 2719
The Man with the Child in His Eyes/Moving	EMI 2806
Hammer Horror/Coffee Homeground	EMI 2887
Wow/Fullhouse	EMI 2911
Breathing/The Empty Bullring	EMI 5058
Babooshka/Ran Tan Waltz	EMI 5085
Army Dreamers/Delius/Passing Through Air	EMI 5106
December Will Be Magic Again/Warm and Soothing	EMI 5121
Sat In Your Lap/Lord of the Reedy River	EMI 5201
The Dreaming/Dreamtime (Instrumental)	EMI 5296
There Goes a Tenner/Ne T'enfuis Pas	EMI 5350
On Stage	MIEP 2991
Ne T'enfuis Pas/Un Baiser D'enfant	EMI 5444

The Whole Story
Wuthering Heights/Cloudbusting/The Man with the Child in His Eyes/Wow/Running Up That Hill/Hounds of Love/Breathing/Army Dreamers/Sat In Your Lap/Experiment IV/The Dreaming/Babooshka

EMI	KBTV1	LP	UK	1986	
EMI	CDP7464142	CD	UK	1986	
EMI	EMS91204	LP	Japan	1986	promo
EMI	EMI10011	LP	Argentina	1986	
Simply Vinyl	SVLP268	LP	UK	2000	180g

This Woman's Work
8CD box set includes all albums plus two CDs of collected tracks.

EMI	CDKBBX1	box set	UK	1990
EMI	TOCP646067	box set	Japan	1990
EMI	CDKBBX1	box set	UK	1998

A Lioness at Heart
Includes CD album of *Lionheart*, 48-page booklet, postcard, t-shirt and poster, limited to 1,000 copies.

EMI	—	box set	UK	1992

ORIGINAL CHART POSITIONS (not including reissues)

Singles

	UK	USA	Australia
Wuthering Heights	1	–	1
The Man with the Child in His Eyes	6	85	–
Hammer Horror	44	–	–
Wow	14	–	–
Breathing	16	–	–
Babooshka	5	–	1
Army Dreamers	16	–	–
December Will Be Magic Again	29	–	–
The Dreaming	48	–	–
Suspended in Gaffa	–	–	10
Running Up That Hill	3	30	–
Cloudbusting	20	–	–
Hounds of Love	18	–	–
The Big Sky	37	–	–
Experiment IV	23	–	–
The Sensual World	12	6	44
This Woman's Work	25	–	–
Love and Anger	38	–	–
Rocket Man	12	11	2
Rubberband Girl	12	88	–
Moments of Pleasure	26	–	–
The Red Shoes	21	–	–
The Man I Love	22	–	–
And So Is Love	26	–	–

Albums

	UK	USA	Australia
The Kick Inside	3	–	–
Lionheart	6	–	–
Never For Ever	1	–	–
The Dreaming	3	157	–

Hounds of Love	1	30	–
The Whole Story	1	74	28
The Sensual World	2	43	25
The Red Shoes	2	28	–

Appendix C

Videography

Individual promotional videos were filmed for all of the following songs (directors in parentheses):

Wuthering Heights (Keith Macmillan, 1978), The Man with the Child in His Eyes (Keith Macmillan, 1978), Hammer Horror (Keith Macmillan, 1978), Wow (Keith Macmillan, 1978), Breathing (Keith Macmillan, 1980), Babooshka (Keith Macmillan, 1980), Army Dreamers (Keith Macmillan, 1980), Sat in Your Lap (Brian Wiseman, 1981), The Dreaming (Paul Henry, 1982), Suspended in Gaffa (Brian Wiseman, 1982), Running Up That Hill (David Garfath, 1985), Cloudbusting (Julian Doyle, 1985), Hounds of Love (Kate Bush, 1985), The Big Sky (Kate Bush, 1986), Experiment IV (Kate Bush, 1986), The Sensual World (Kate Bush and Peter Richardson, 1989), This Woman's Work (Kate Bush, 1989), Love and Anger (Kate Bush, 1990), Rocket Man (Kate Bush, 1991), Rubberband Girl (1993), Moments of Pleasure (1993), The Red Shoes (1993), And So Is Love (1994).

The following video compilations have been released:

The Single File (Picture Music, 1983)
Wuthering Heights/The Man with the Child in His Eyes/Hammer Horror/Wow/Them Heavy People/Breathing/Babooshka/Army Dreamers/Sat in Your Lap/The Dreaming/Suspended in Gaffa/There Goes a Tenner.

The Whole Story (Picture Music International, 1986)
Wuthering Heights/Cloudbusting/The Man with the Child in His Eyes/Breathing/Wow/Hounds of Love/Running Up That Hill/Army

Dreamers/Sat in Your Lap/Experiment IV/The Dreaming/Babooshka/The Big Sky.

Hair of the Hound **(Picture Music International, 1986)**
Features 'Running Up That Hill', 'Hounds of Love', 'Cloudbusting' and 'The Big Sky'.

The Sensual World **(Picture Music International, 1990)**
Includes an interview with Kate plus the promo clips for 'The Sensual World', 'Love and Anger' and 'This Woman's Work'.

The following live video has been released:

Live at Hammersmith Odeon **(Picture Music, 1981)**
Filmed on 13 May 1979: Moving/Them Heavy People/Violin/Strange Phenomena/Hammer Horror/Don't Push Your Foot on the Heartbrake/Wow/Feel It/Kite/James and the Cold Gun/Oh England, My Lionheart/Wuthering Heights.

The following film has been released:

The Line, The Cross & The Curve **(Picture Music International, 1994)**
Includes the songs 'Rubberband Girl', 'And So Is Love', 'The Red Shoes', 'Lily', 'Moments of Pleasure' and 'Eat the Music'. The cast features Kate Bush, Miranda Richardson, Lindsay Kemp, Lily, Stewart Arnold and Peter Richardson.

Bibliography

The following books, journals, fanzines and websites were most helpful in researching this book.

BOOKS

Bolton, Cecil (ed.), *The Best of Kate Bush*, EMI, London, 1981

Cann, Kevin, and Mayes, Sean, *Kate Bush A Visual Documentary*, Omnibus Press, London, 1988

Gambaccini, Paul, Rice, Tim, and Rice, Jonathan, *British Hit Albums*, Guinness, London, 1994

Gambaccini, Paul, Rice, Tim, and Rice, Jonathan, *British Hit Singles*, Guinness, London, 1995

Gray, Michael, Lazell, Barry, and Osbourne, Roger, *30 Years of NME Album Charts*, Boxtree, London, 1993

Juby, Kerry, *Kate Bush*, Sidgwick & Jackson, London, 1988

Kerton, Paul, *Kate Bush – An Illustrated Biography*, Proteus, London, 1980

Rees, Dafydd, and Crampton, Luke, *Q Rock Stars Encyclopedia*, Dorling Kindersley, London, 1999

Vermorel, Fred, *The Secret History of Kate Bush*, Omnibus Press, London, 1983

Vermorel, Fred and Judy, *Kate Bush Biography*, Target Books, London, 1979

Whelton, Carmel, *Never Forever*, UFO Books, London, 1992

PERIODICALS

Associated Press, *Billboard*, *Company*, *Daily Express*, *Daily Mail*, *Daily Mirror*, *Electronic Soundmaker & Computer Music*, *Electronics & Music Maker*, *Guardian*, *i-D*, *Independent*, *International Musician*, Kate Bush Club Newsletters (1979–1993), *Keyboard*, *Melody Maker*, *New Musical Express*, *Observer*, *Option*, *PopPix*, *Popular Video*, *Practical Hi-Fi, Q*, *Record Collector*, *Record Mirror*, *Rolling Stone*, *Scotsman*, *Select*, *Smash Hits*, *Spin*, *Sounds*, *Sun*, *Daily Telegraph*, *The Times* (London), *Uncut*, *Video Times*, *Voice and Vox*.

FANZINES

Homeground, 1983–2005, edited by Krystyna Fitzgerald-Morris, Peter Fitzgerald-Morris and David Cross. Contact PO Box 439, Rochester, Kent, ME3 8WE, England.
Under the Ivy, issues 1–4.

ONLINE SOURCES

Many online sites cover the life, music and art of Kate Bush. Some of the best are:

http://gaffa.org/intro/toc.html

http://homepage.eircom.net/~twoms/homegrou.htm

http://homepage.eircom.net/~twoms/katenews.htm

http://www.katebush.info/home.php?link=txt/clubs.htm

Hunt around, there's a lot of material out there.

Thanks and Acknowledgements

As usual, there have been many people who have helped to various degrees and in many different ways with the preparation of this book. My principal thanks go to the musicians and collaborators who took time out from their busy schedules to chat with me and answer my ever-lengthening list of questions: Ian Bairnson, Kevin Burke, Tina Earnshaw, Nick Launay, Pat Martin, Max Middleton, Charlie Morgan, Hugh Padgham, David Paton and Alan Skidmore, plus all the others who wished to remain anonymous.

Thanks for support and encouragement as usual to my wife Carolyn, to Gino Farabella, Graham Palmer and Rob North, to Krystyna Fitzgerald-Morris, Peter Fitzgerald-Morris and David Cross at the excellent *Homeground* magazine, to Seán at the *Kate Bush News & Information* website and everyone else who emailed in their stories and anecdotes, including Darrell Babidge and Mark Binmore, and a special thanks to David Sheasby for the use of his photos.

Kate Bush material was pretty much all put to use from my own collection, so maybe I should thank all the sellers on eBay who have helped by taking my money over the years! Also thanks to Clive Whichelow at Backnumbers, 'Rantan4ever' for the DVDS, all the Kate Bush websites, Francis Monkman, Karen Pinegar, Kay Skidmore and Simon Dix, and to Aileen for a lovely week at her cottage on Arran!

Last, but definitely not least, I'd like to thank everyone at Piatkus books for making this book happen, especially Alice Davis for commissioning it and providing a guiding hand, and also to Alison Sturgeon and Victoria Wilson. I know they must have felt as if they were waiting for the next Kate Bush album at times instead of this book. If indeed this has taken as long as one of Kate's albums it must be one of her early ones.

Author's Note

As well as the sources documented in the bibliography there were a myriad Kate Bush interviews used in researching this book. Radio shows and interviews, TV programmes, press conferences and press releases cover just some of the other sources that I consulted. In every case I contacted (or left messages with) the person concerned directly, and only if they were unable to participate did I use secondary source material. The new interviews I carried out during 2004 and early 2005 (in fact, the last interview was conducted on the day of my deadline) added much to the manuscript and my thanks for these are elsewhere.

Index